THE DYNAMICS OF LITURGY

D. Vincent Twomey, S.V.D.

THE DYNAMICS
OF LITURGY

Joseph Ratzinger's
Theology of Liturgy: An Interpretation

IGNATIUS PRESS   SAN FRANCISCO

Cover design by Roxanne Mei Lum

© 2022 by Ignatius Press, San Francisco
All rights reserved
ISBN 978-1-62164-486-6 (PB)
ISBN 978-1-64229-225-1 (eBook)
Library of Congress Control number 2022933391
Printed in the United States of America ∞

True theology is always living, a form of hierugy,
something that changes our life
and "assumes" us into itself:
we are to become theology.
Understood in this way,
theology is not a matter for specialists
but a universal vocation;
each is called to become a "theologian soul".

— Archimandrite Vasileios

CONTENTS

PREFACE

The term "dynamic" is characteristic of Ratzinger's theology, the basic impulse of which, he once said, "was always to free up the authentic kernel of the faith from encrustations and to give this kernel strength and dynamism".[1] The term can refer to the dynamism of grace—"the inner dynamic of gift with which the Lord renews us and draws us into what is his"[2]—or to what it means to be a Christian: "the entire dynamic of 'being for'."[3] It can refer to "the dynamic of mission"[4] as well as to the interior dynamism of the Resurrection as the interior locus of Christian worship.[5] He also speaks about the "dynamic of faith", which is lacking in a Church that is preoccupied with structures.[6] In accord with the theological axiom *gratia supponet naturam*, God's transformative action in the embodied soul presupposes an intrinsic capacity to be transformed. In other words, there is, corresponding to the dynamism of grace, a dynamism intrinsic to our created human nature

[1] Joseph Cardinal Ratzinger, *Salt of the Earth: The Church at the End of the Millennium. An Interview with Peter Seewald*, trans. Adrian Walker (San Francisco: Ignatius Press, 1997), 79.

[2] See, for example, his *Jesus of Nazareth*, part 2, *Holy Week: From the Entrance into Jerusalem to the Resurrection* (London/San Francisco: Catholic Truth Society/ Ignatius Press, 2011), 62.

[3] Ibid., 88; cf. also 86.

[4] Ibid., 98.

[5] Cf. ibid., 144.

[6] Cf. Peter Seewald, *Benedikt XVI. Ein Leben* (Munich: Droemer, 2020), 667–68.

open to God, namely, man's natural religiosity (as distinct from faith). It is an aspect of what Pope Benedict XVI called "the inner dynamic of [natural] religion toward self-transcendence, which involves a search for truth".[7] That inner dynamic finds its initial expression in ritual, which has its own inbuilt dynamics. It is these ritual dynamics (plural) that will be our main focus in what follows. But first, it will be necessary to fill in the historical background to what has become known as the Benedictine Reform, or the Reform of the Reform mandated by the Second Vatican Council, by taking a brief look at the reasons why the council decided that the ancient Roman Rite needed to be reformed in the first place. And in conclusion, an attempt will be made to situate the reform of the liturgy in the salvific-historical epoch inaugurated by the council. It must be admitted that the following essays concentrate on the ritual of the Eucharist, even though, as Cardinal Koch once reminded the participants at a conference in Rome on the liturgy, such a concentration fails to do justice either to the liturgical reality in the life of the Church or to the basic theological-liturgical impulse of Vatican II.[8] However, I am convinced that the basic insights into the dynamics of the liturgy are applicable to the entire gamut

[7] Benedict XVI, *Jesus of Nazareth. The Infancy Narratives* (New York: Image, 2012), 95.

[8] Kurt Cardinal Koch, "Gabe und Aufgabe: Roms Liturgiereformen in ökumenischer Perspektive", in Stephan Heid, ed., *Operation am lebenden Objekt: Roms Liturgiereformen von Trient bis zum Vaticanum II* (Berlin, 2014), 11. A similar observation was made by Aidan Kavanagh, "Relevance and Change in the Liturgy", *Worship* 45/2 (1971): 58–72, where he draws attention to the two fundamental sacraments—baptism and Eucharist—which form the axis around which all the other sacraments and their liturgical celebration take place. The neglect of the significance of baptism in particular can lead to empty ritualism, be it progressive or traditionalist, and a false, i.e., exclusive, concentration on the Eucharist.

of liturgical celebrations as well as to the Divine Office when sung or recited in choir.

Apart from the excursus, chapter 6, and an appendix on the spirituality of sacred chant, the other chapters originated as introductory papers read to the *Fota International Liturgical Conferences 2008–2012*, Cork, Ireland, organized by Monsignor James O'Brien, who at the time was an official in the Congregation for Divine Worship and the Discipline of the Sacraments. First published as part of the proceedings of the conference, they have been revised for this publication. There is no attempt to present a full account of Ratzinger's theology of liturgy.[9] Rather, this collection of essays is an interpretation of central aspects of that theology and is aimed at encouraging the reader to study Ratzinger's original theology. Though generally ignored by professional liturgists, Ratzinger has much, I am convinced, to contribute to the recovery of the authentic dynamics of Divine Worship and, so, to a worthy celebration of the sacraments, which profoundly affects the lives of priests and faithful alike beyond the confines of academia.

When teaching the tract on the sacraments in the Holy Spirit Seminary of Papua New Guinea and the Solomon

---

[9] Such is to be found in Mariusz Biliniewicz, *The Liturgical Vision of Pope Benedict XVI: A Theological Inquiry* (Oxford: Peter Lang, 2013), also for the most recent literature; I should like to highlight the following in particular: Emery de Gaál, *The Theology of Pope Benedict XVI: The Christocentric Shift* (New York: Palgrave Macmillan, 2010), 239–67; Neil J. Roy and Janet E. Rutherford, eds., *Benedict XVI and the Sacred Liturgy: Proceedings of the First Fota International Conference* (Dublin: Four Courts Press, 2010); Aidan Nichols, O.P., *The Thought of Pope Benedict XVI: An Introduction to the Theology of Joseph Ratzinger*, new ed. (London and New York: Burns & Oates, 2007), 147–59; Joseph Murphy, *Christ Our Joy: The Theological Vision of Pope Benedict XVI* (San Francisco: Ignatius Press, 2008), 171–83; Siegfried Wiedenhofer, *Die Theologie Joseph Ratzingers / Benedikt XVI: Ein Blick auf das Ganze* (Regensburg: Verlag Friedrich Pustet, 2016), 646–54.

Islands, I was first confronted with the question of the nature of ritual. My confrere Father James Knight, S.V.D., guided me in my study of the anthropology of ritual, for which I am most grateful. However, it was Monsignor O'Brien's invitation to chair the Fota International Liturgical Conferences devoted to the "Benedictine Reform" that challenged me to put my thoughts down on paper. I remain most grateful to him for the opportunity not only to deliver the opening address but also to make the acquaintance, and to learn from, some of the world's leading liturgists and theologians, whom he invited to the conference. I also thank him for permission to use the texts that were originally published in the Proceedings of the Fota Conference. My thanks are also due to Carl Olsen, for permission to publish the article on the Amazon Rite that first appeared in *Catholic World Report*, May 20, 2020. I wish to thank those who read sections of the following chapters and made valuable criticisms and suggestions: Mark Bennett, John Hogan, Mary Lynch, Dermot Fenlon, Martin Trimpe, and Seán MacGiollarnáth, O.Carm. I am grateful to Tim Cunningham for his permission to use his poem "Tabernacle". Special thanks are due to Father Joseph D. Fessio, S.J., and to the editorial board and staff of Ignatius Press for accepting the manuscript for publication. In particular, I should like to thank Anne Nash, Emily Ayala, and Laura Peredo for their patience and professionalism.

How can I express my gratitude to the inspiration proved by my former teacher's profound theology? I fear that I may not have done justice to his thought, but I hope nonetheless that the following chapters will spur the reader on to return to his writings, to discover for oneself the theological depth that has yet to be plumbed. Finally, this little book is dedicated to my first-ever students, the seminarians of Papua New Guinea and the Solomon Islands, whose fresh and vibrant faith combined with eager and open minds awakening to theology stimulated me to find answers to the profound questions they raised in seminars, tutorials, and class discussions.

Donamon, County Roscommon
Feast of the Epiphany, 2022

INTRODUCTION

Why the Reform of the Liturgy?

Liturgy involves our understanding of God and the world and our relationship to Christ, the Church, and ourselves. How we attend to liturgy determines the fate of the faith and the Church.

—Joseph Ratzinger, *A New Song for the Lord*

When Pope Saint John XXIII called the Second Vatican Council, a number of leading European cardinals were invited to an unofficial meeting in Genoa in 1961 to discuss how they should approach the forthcoming council. Cardinal Frings, Archbishop of Cologne, asked Joseph Ratzinger, recently appointed Professor of Fundamental Theology at the University of Bonn, to ghostwrite the paper he was to give in Genoa.[1] Unlike the previous council, Vatican II was not convoked to address a particular set

---

[1] The original German text, "Das Konzil und die moderne Gedankenwelt", is reproduced in *Joseph Ratzinger Gesammelte Schriften* [= *JRGS*], ed. Gerhard Ludwig Müller, vol. 7/1 (Freiburg, 2012), 73–91. From henceforth, all references to Pope Benedict XVI/Joseph Cardinal Ratzinger will be simply given as Ratzinger, except for his magisterial teachings, for which his papal title is used. See Peter Seewald, *Benedikt XVI: Ein Leben* (Munich: Droemer, 2020), 378–91, for a detailed description of the origin and the content of, as well as the profound impact made by, this, "the most important and most influential speech Ratzinger ever wrote" (382). According to Seewald, John XXIII even incorporated some of Ratzinger's ideas into his opening address to the council (cf. 383–84).

of problems with doctrine or even with outright heresy. There was an awareness at the time of the serious decline in the influence of the Church on human affairs and in the lives of people. This is as serious as heresy, even if the malaise is of a less evident kind.[2] For that reason, Pope Saint John XXIII summed up the task he set for the council as *aggiornamento* [bringing up to date]. What was the cause of that malaise?

Ratzinger, at the very start of his career as a theologian, had already published a paper in 1958 entitled "The New Pagans and the Church". In it, he claimed that so-called Christian Europe had in fact over the past four centuries brought forth from its midst a new heathenism. It was a deceptive and dangerous kind of heathenism, since it was born in the Church herself and "has borrowed from her the essential elements that definitely determine its outward form and its power".[3] At a conservative estimate, more than half of baptized Catholics no longer practice. They have an à-la-carte approach to the Church's Creed. Their philosophy is a secular one, while their ethics are purely rational and irreligious. They can no longer be called believers. Since lack of faith can be presumed in most people we meet, then this has two

[2] Father Seán MacGiollarnáth, O.Carm., email dated October 27, 2020.
[3] "Die neue Heiden und die Kirche", *Hochland* 51 (1958/59): 1–11; English translation by Kenneth Baker, S.J., in *Homiletic and Pastoral Review*, January 13, 2017. He added: "One should speak rather about the much more characteristic phenomenon of our time, which determines the real attack against the Christian, [namely, an attack] from the paganism within the Church herself, from the 'desolating sacrilege set up where it ought not to be' (Mk 13:14)." This essay was, according to Seewald, his first significant, controversial publication, which almost brought his career as a theologian to an end: see Seewald, *Benedikt XVI: Ein Leben*, 313–22. Seewald claims that this "essay can be seen as a harbinger of that tremor, which broke out at the Second Vatican Council as a lava-spewing eruption" (319).

serious consequences: it calls into question the fundamental structures of the Church, and it produces an essential change of consciousness among still-believing Christians.[4] The new heathenism threatens both our understanding of the Church and her mission as well as the existential well-being of practicing Catholics. Ratzinger was not alone in his concerns. There were others, such as Dorothy Day and Catholic intellectual figures like George Bernanos, who also raised the alarm.[5]

In his paper intended for the meeting of cardinals in Genoa, Ratzinger defines *aggiornamento* as "carefully scrutinizing the intellectual world of today, within which [the forthcoming council] should place the lampstand of the Gospel, so that its light does not remain under a bushel of antiquated forms but, unmistakably, will rather illuminate all those who live in the house of our times (Mt 5:15)."[6] After an introductory *tour d'horizon* of the changes in the intellectual/cultural situation since the First Vatican Council,[7] the body of the essay uncovers the different layers that make up the cultural situation of the world on the eve of the council. The first layer is the experience of the unity of mankind (thanks, e.g., to modern communications and

[4] This could be summed up in the question: Why should I be a Christian, if others can be saved without being Christian, since the [false] understanding of *salus extra ecclesiam non est* (there is no salvation outside the [visible] Church) was no longer perceived to be convincing?

[5] See the valuable article by Larry Chapp, "The Constantinian Heathenism of the Church: Joseph Ratzinger and the Crisis of Our Time", *Gaudium et Spes* 22, February 3, 2021.

[6] "Das Konzil und die moderne Gedankenwelt", 73.

[7] He concluded his *tour d'horizon* with the assertion that the seeds of the intellectual threats to the faith that were sown in the nineteenth century had, in the meantime, ripened into full maturity by the middle of the twentieth; cf. Philip Trower, *Turmoil & Truth: The Historical Roots of the Modern Crisis in the Catholic Church* (Oxford and San Francisco: Family Publications and Ignatius Press, 2003).

transport). "All mankind thinks and speaks in the categories of the technological civilization of an European-American character, with the result that mankind as a whole has entered into a stage of unification, which is comparable to that which, at the time of Jesus, had been reached in the Mediterranean basin thanks to the unifying culture of Hellenism."[8] This historically new situation, today known as globalization, offers the Church new possibilities, since the Catholica by its very nature has been from the outset fundamentally intended for the whole of mankind. Just as early Christianity adapted and transformed the common dialect of the day—Koine Greek—with all its pagan philosophical assumptions to enable it convincingly to proclaim the message of Jesus Christ, the task the Church faces today is to use, and to mold, the homogeneous thought and language of today's technical civilization into a new Christian dialect for the world.

On the other hand, the horrors of the two world wars waged by so-called Christian nations revealed to the world the dark possibilities of European culture and understandably evoked in the non-Christian world a profound skepticism toward Christianity—together with a new appreciation of their own specific national cultures and religious traditions. This it did, paradoxically, despite their own embrace of the universal technological civilization of "Western" provenance. The newfound confidence (and universal claims) of Eastern religions and of Islam has had a disillusioning effect on European self-confidence and, with it, the absolute claims of Christianity. Relativism is the inevitable outcome. Despite the positive values in relativism—such as a reciprocal modesty about one's claims and the promotion of a greater understanding

---

[8] "Das Konzil und die moderne Gedankenwelt", 77 (own translation).

between peoples—the task for the forthcoming council should be to liberate what is truly absolute in Christianity from what appear to be absolute but in fact are historically changeable forms and institutions. This demands of the Church that she be more open than heretofore "to the whole gamut of the human spirit that behooves her as the Catholica, which the Fathers liked to compare with the Bride, about whom the Psalmist says she is surrounded by multi-colored apparel (Ps 44:10 Vg)."⁹

At a deeper level, Ratzinger then goes on to analyze the effect of modern technology on human consciousness. As a product of man's creativity in response to the Creator's mandate to till the earth (Gen 2:15), technology is basically to be welcomed. However, as a result of the dominance of technology in every aspect of life, man is no longer in direct contact with his natural environment—God's work—but only with his own work, and so has become preoccupied with self and alienated from God. Modern atheism is a side effect of the industrial revolution.

> That also means, however, that the new heathenism that developed within the heart of the Christian world during the last century is basically different from its earlier form: there are no more gods; rather, the world is irreversibly stripped of its gods, it has become profane, with man alone still standing in the clearing. Now, indeed, he senses a kind of religious reverence for mankind itself or at least for that part of mankind to which technical progress is indebted.¹⁰

In a word: the religious situation of mankind has been altered radically.

⁹ Ibid., 80.
¹⁰ Ibid., 82–83

The Church's most urgent task is to expound anew her enduring claim on mankind in this changed situation. How this is to be done demands, first of all, a reflection on the generally accepted faith in science to regulate life. Ever since Auguste Comte, every aspect of human life, personal and collective, has been the subject of scientific study with the aim of establishing scientifically what is human and how we humans should behave. Only against this background, Ratzinger comments, can the Kinsey Report with its claim to derive behavioral norms from statistical evidence be understood. Likewise, the findings of psychology as applied in various psychotherapeutic practices are now expected to heal disturbed functional systems without recourse to such loaded terms as guilt and sin.

However, man remains what Augustine calls "the great abyss". While the various human sciences can indeed help in various ways, ultimately the human person remains beyond the grasp of every science.

> Love remains the great miracle that evades all calcula-
> tion; guilt remains the dark possibility that no statistic can
> discuss away, and at the bottom of the human heart that
> loneliness remains which yearns for infinity itself and can
> in the last analysis be stilled by nothing else because that
> word endures: "solo dios basta"—infinity alone suffices
> for man, whose measure is once again established as noth-
> ing less than what is unlimited.[11]

This needs to be articulated in such a way that the modern world can appreciate and embrace the ultimate answers to the deepest yearnings of the human heart that Christianity offers, perennial truths that today have become

---

[11] Ibid., 84.

unrecognizable because they are couched in historically conditioned formulas and practices.

Finally, Ratzinger examines the various ideologies—especially, but not only, the dominant ideologies of Marxism and neoliberalism—that attempt to give an overall meaning to life; they also offer a *collective* vision of hope for mankind, now that religion is no longer seen as providing either meaning or hope. He warns his hearers that the Christianity of the past century, by concentrating perhaps too much on the salvation of individual souls that is to be found in the hereafter, may have failed to speak loudly enough about the salvation of the world itself, about the universal hope of Christianity.[12] Above all, our contemporaries, who imagine that Catholics must unquestionably accept truths imposed on them from above, must recognize in Catholicism a genuine struggle to come to terms with the most important intellectual issues facing mankind today.

In conclusion, Ratzinger reminds his listeners that the Church still lives as ever under the breath of the Holy Spirit, who inspires movements of renewal in the Church apart from the apostolic authorities. To illustrate this, he comments on what he calls two main charismatic movements within the Church over the past century, namely, the Marian Movement symbolized by Lourdes and Fatima, on the one hand, and the Liturgical Movement, on the other. Both were devotional movements that spontaneously emerged from the base, as it were, but were in time recognized and, in various degrees, adopted by the hierarchy. "Liturgical piety is, to use a rather imprecise slogan, objective-sacramental; Marian piety, subjective-personal; liturgical piety obeys the law 'per Christum ad patrem', while Marian piety says 'per Mariam ad

[12] Cf. ibid., 87.

Jesum'."[13] There are many other differences, even to the predominance of one or other according to geographical regions. The task for the future is to enable them reciprocally to fructify each other. Commenting on geographical differences, Ratzinger draws attention to the multiplicity of nations, whose culture and history constitute the richness of the Church, "since each brings its specific charism into the unity of the Church", and he adds: "today we can scarcely surmise which new richness will accrue to the Church when the charisms of Asia and Africa appear on the horizon."[14] This statement has enormous implications for the postconciliar reform of the liturgy.

Frings was so impressed with what the young professor had proposed that he made but one small change in the text before delivering it on November 20, 1961. The following February, while attending a meeting of the official Preparatory Commission in Rome, Cardinal Frings was surprised to be summoned to a private audience by Pope John XXIII, who the night before had read Ratzinger's speech.[15] The cardinal feared that his proposals for the council might have displeased the pope, but, to his own surprise, he was greeted warmly with the words: "Thank you, your Eminence, you said the very things I wanted to

[13] Ibid., 90.

[14] Ibid. Ratzinger ends his paper by drawing attention to the astonishing phenomenon of contemporary Christian martyrs, numerically more than all the martyrs of the Roman persecutions during the first three centuries of the Church, and he asks rhetorically: "How can we still fancy ourselves to be godforsaken, when living in a century that is capable of producing such witnesses? How can we complain about the lack of faith and tiredness of the Church? That the Church is still, and more so than ever, a Church of martyrs is the guarantee that the power of the Holy Spirit still lives in her without interruption. The mark of suffering is the mark of its unconquerable life. To serve this life will be the task of the forthcoming council" (ibid., 91).

[15] The Italian translation used by Cardinal Frings had been published in the Genoese periodical, *Spirit and Life*.

say myself, but I could not find the words."[16] As a result, Frings invited Ratzinger (aged thirty-five) to accompany him to the council as his *peritus* (theological expert adviser), thus positioning Ratzinger to be a major influence on the teaching of the Second Vatican Council.

Pope Benedict XVI recalled this incident in his address to the parish priests and clergy of Rome on February 14, 2013, shortly before he relinquished the Petrine Office. In the same address, Pope Benedict, speaking without notes, proffered "a few thoughts" on the council—in fact, what he did was typical of how he usually approached a topic as a professor. He first offered a synthetic overview of the council's deliberations before going on to suggest a critical evaluation of what he judged to be the most important texts, not least due to their postconciliar significance, namely, the Declaration on Religious Freedom (*Dignitatis Humanae*) and the Declaration on the Relation of the Church to Non-Christian Religions (*Nostra Aetate*). He concluded that address with some comments on the reception of the council in the wake of the historic event. In that reception, he noted, the media had played a prominent role during the council, a phenomenon that was new to conciliar history.[17] The nature of such reporting by journalists with little or no theological training and whose métier is that of political life could not, with the best will in the world, but present a more-or-less distorted message to the general public (including the clergy) as compared to what in fact had been intended by the Council Fathers. "[On the one hand] there was the Council of the

[16] Cf. Jared Wicks, "Six Texts by Prof. Joseph Ratzinger as *peritus* before and during Vatican Council II", *Gregorianum* 89 (2008): 233–311, here 234–35.

[17] See D. Vincent Twomey, S.V.D., "The Second Vatican Council: An Irish Perspective", *Studies: An Irish Quarterly Review*, 101 (2012): 407–22, in particular 409–11.

Fathers—the real Council—but [on the other hand] there was also the Council of the media." He continued:

> It was almost a Council apart, and the world perceived the Council through the latter, through the media. Thus, the Council that reached the people with immediate effect was that of the media, not that of the Fathers. And while the Council of the Fathers was conducted within the faith—it was a Council of faith seeking *intellectus*, seeking to understand itself and seeking to understand the signs of God at that time, seeking to respond to the challenge of God at that time and to find in the word of God a word for today and tomorrow—while all the Council, as I said, moved within the faith, as *fides quaerens intellectum*, the Council of the journalists, naturally, was not conducted within the faith, but within the categories of today's media, namely, apart from faith, with a different hermeneutic. It was a political hermeneutic: for the media, the Council was a political struggle, a power struggle between different trends in the Church. It was obvious that the media would take the side of those who seemed to them more closely allied with their world.[18]

Indeed, the influence of the media's spin on the implementation—especially the reformed liturgy—cannot be underestimated.

ᖥ ᖥ ᖥ

What did the council intend? In his Christmas Address to the College of Cardinals and the members of the Roman Curia on December 22, 2005, Pope Benedict XVI commented, among other things, on the fortieth anniversary

[18] Pope Benedict XVI, Meeing with the Parish Priests and Clergy of Rome, February 14, 2013.

of the closing of the Second Vatican Council, which had been celebrated that year. He recalled how the reception of the council had been greatly influenced by those who interpreted the council as marking a radical discontinuity with the Church's tradition. The so-called spirit of the council was preferred to the actual documents themselves to justify innovations that were not foreseen, much less approved, by the council. But, he countered, the bishops had no authority to change the Church's nature so radically. Thanks to the sacrament they received, bishops "are 'stewards of the mysteries of God' (I Cor 4:1); as such, they must be found to be 'faithful' and 'wise' (cf. Lk 12:41–48)." He refers to a number of Gospel parables, which "express the dynamic of fidelity required in the Lord's service; and through them it becomes clear that, as in a Council, the dynamic and fidelity must converge." It cannot be denied that "this synthesis of fidelity and dynamic is demanding", but it is precisely that synthesis which constitutes the hermeneutics of reform, as originally intended by Pope Saint John XXIII, when he called the council.[19]

꒰ꔧ ꒰ꔧ ꒰ꔧ

The Council Fathers themselves outlined what they had hoped the council would achieve in the opening lines of *Sacrosanctum Concilium*: the Constitution on the Sacred Liturgy (hereafter abbreviated *SC*)—a programmatic

[19] For a comprehensive discussion of the issues raised by this document, see Papst Benedikt XVI. und Sein Schülerkreis, Kurt Kardinal Koch, *Das Zweite Vatikanische Konzil: Die Hermeneutik der Reform* (Augsburg: Sankt Ulrich, 2021); see also Kurt Cardinal Koch, "Gabe und Aufgabe: Roms Liturgiereformen in ökumenischer Perspektive", in Stephan Heid, ed., *Operation am lebenden Objekt: Roms Liturgiereformen von Trient bis zum Vaticanum II* (Berlin, 2014, 11–26).

statement, setting the agenda for the council: The Sacred
Council has set out

1. to impart an ever-increasing vigor to the Christian
   life of the faithful;
2. to adapt more closely to the needs of our age those
   institutions that are subject to change;
3. to foster whatever can promote union among all
   who believe in Christ;
4. to strengthen whatever can help to call all mankind
   into the Church's fold.

In a word, Vatican II's primary purpose was missionary, to reinvigorate the Church's divine mission to bring
salvation to all mankind—so that all would become one
in Christ—and to achieve this by promoting an interior
renewal of the Church as communion.[20] The renewal
of the liturgy was to be central to that interior renewal;
indeed, it should become the dynamic driving force of the
Church's mission.[21] As the Council Fathers affirm: "For
the liturgy is the outstanding means whereby the faithful may express in their lives, and manifest to others, the
mystery of Christ and the real nature of the true Church"
(SC 2). The interior renewal of the faithful, and their consequent engagement in the mission of the Church, should
be the ultimate test of all authentic reform of the liturgy.
Did the renewed liturgy impart "an ever-increasing vigor
to the Christian life of the faithful"? That is the question
that can only be answered in the local Churches throughout

[20] The Church as communion (a term, it must be added, not found here in
the text) has, in more recent years, become the favorite model for understanding the Church in the light of the council.

[21] The preceding text had stated: "The Council therefore sees particularly
cogent reasons for undertaking the reform and promotion [instaurandam et
fovendam] of the liturgy."

the world. But it is worth stressing that this first criterion is the overarching aim of all authentic reform. The other three criteria are intrinsically ordered to it.

The second criterion could be formulated as follows: To what extent is the renewed liturgy truly adapted "to the needs of our own times"—that is, in the age of globalization? In other words, can a newly reformed liturgy touch the hearts and minds of our contemporaries in their diverse cultural contexts so as to help draw them close to Christ? This criterion is perhaps the most difficult to establish, in the first instance, because of the diversity of local cultures, many of which, such as those of Asia or Africa, have their own symbolic and ritual languages, which, should they enrich the liturgy, must be subject to a process of purification, inner transformation, and elevation, as Ratzinger has often pointed out. But this difficulty is exacerbated due to the increasingly dominant cultural forces unleashed by the ever increasing, worldwide influence of the Western secular, technological mentality. Whatever benefits they bring, the spread of Western science and technology, with its underlying rationalism, utilitarianism, and materialism, tend to stifle the spiritual needs of people everywhere, Christian and non-Christian alike.[22] In addition, they also rob the indigenous religious traditions of their own unique spiritual and moral depth, leading to a descent into the dark world of magic and superstition.[23] And, of course, it

[22] H. J. J. M. van Straelen, S.V.D., *The Church and the Non-Christian Religions at the Threshold of the 21st Century: A Historical and Theological Study* (London: Avon Books, 1998), gives a good insight into the complexity of inculturation—or, to use the more accurate term that Ratzinger coined, interculturation (see his "Christ, Faith and the Challenge of Cutures", *Origins*, 24 [1995]: 679–86)—and he does so within the existential context of a modernity that now covers the globe, thanks to modern communication possibilities and increased education.

[23] See Ratzinger, *Truth and Tolerance: Christian Belief and World Religions*, trans. Henry Taylor (San Francisco: Ignatius Press, 2004), 76–77.

is to the spiritual needs of people that the reformed liturgy must be adapted.

The third criterion is: that the renewed liturgy should foster "union among all who believe in Christ". Ecumenism, which was one of the great concerns of the council, might seem irrelevant to the reform of the liturgy, but is it? Perhaps we can get a clue as to its relevance from a most unexpected source: *Dominus Iesus*. There is but one, holy, and apostolic Church, the declaration makes clear, and it "subsists in" the Catholic Church, that is, local churches in communion with the successor of Saint Peter. Catholic here has its original meaning, i.e., all-embracing or inclusive. This means that the liturgy should, to some degree, reflect this inclusive understanding of the Church. In other words, the reform must, in some real sense, be such that Orthodox, Anglican, Protestant, and Evangelical Christians can, to the extent that they share the essential characteristics of the One, Holy, Catholic, and Apostolic Church find an echo of their own forms of worship. But the other side of the coin is the possibility of the Latin or Roman Rite finding inspiration in, and being enriched by, elements of the liturgies of other Christian churches and ecclesial communities.[24] Further, it should be stressed, liturgists at the time of the council and for decades afterward were ignorant of the ethnographic discoveries regarding the nature of ritual itself, which, had they known about them at the time, could have enabled them to avoid some of the worst liturgical aberrations in the postconciliar reform.[25] This is a major theme, to which we will return.

---

[24] See in particular Cardinal Koch's reflections on the reform of the liturgy from an ecumenical perspective: Koch, "Gabe und Aufgabe", 19–26.

[25] The postconciliar, clerical attitude to liturgy was summed up by Mary Douglas, *Natural Symbols: Explorations in Cosmology* (London: Barrie and Rockliff, Cresset Press, 1970), 4, as follows: "When I ask my clerical friends why

The fourth and final criterion seems to be even more irrelevant to the liturgy as generally experienced today in the West, namely, that any reform should "strengthen whatever can help to call the whole of mankind into the household of the Church" (*SC* 1). How, in the world characterized by technology and globalization, can this aim be achieved? The short answer is: beauty. Cardinal Burke once pointed to the absolutely central relevance of this criterion in a paper he read to the *Third Fota International Liturgical Conference* in 2009 entitled "The New Evangelization and Sacred Music: The Unbroken Continuity of Holiness, Beauty and Universality".[26] According to Cardinal Burke, "The living of our faith with new engagement and new energy, with the engagement and energy of the first disciples and of the first missionaries to various parts of the world, will find its highest expression in the manner of our worship of God, in the various elements of the sacred liturgy."[27]

---

the new forms are held superior, I am answered by a Teilhardist evolutionism which assumes that a rational, verbally explicit, personal commitment to God is self-evidently more evolved and better than its alleged contrary, formal, ritualistic conformity. Questioning this, I am told that ritual conformity is not a valid form of personal commitment and is not compatible with the full development of the personality; also that the replacement of ritual conformity with rational commitment will give greater meaning to the lives of Christians. Furthermore if Christianity is to be saved for future generations, ritualism must be rooted out, as if it were a weed choking the life of the spirit. We find in all this a mood which closely parallels the anti-ritualism which has inspired so many evangelical sects. There is no need to go back to the Reformation to recognize the wave on which these modern Catholics are rather incongruously riding." Moreover, Douglas is at pains to demonstrate that "The contrast of secular with religious has nothing whatever to do with the contrast of modern with traditional or primitive. The idea that primitive man is by nature deeply religious is nonsense. The truth is that all the varieties of scepticism, materialism and spiritual fervour are to be found in the range of tribal societies" (ibid., 18).

[26] In Janet E. Rutherford, ed., *Benedict XVI and Beauty in Sacred Music: Proceedings of the Third Fota International Liturgical Conference* (Dublin and New York: Four Courts Press and Sceptre Publishers, 2012), 24–40.

[27] Ibid., 38.

One is reminded of Solzhenitsyn's quote from Dosto-yevsky in his speech on the occasion of receiving the Nobel Prize for literature (1970): "The world will be saved by beauty", which Solzhenitsyn interpreted to mean that when truth and goodness are banished, then beauty will save the world.[28] In other words, when a culture sup-presses truth, when public discourse is dominated by lies, propaganda, and ideologies, and when goodness—i.e., justice and charity—is banished from society as under a totalitarian regime, then beauty, the creative work of poets, writers, artists, and musicians, will save society, will save mankind.[29]

Worship (cult) is the source of some of the greatest expressions of art in all its manifestations. One should say more accurately that liturgy itself ought to be beauty incar-nate in rite and ritual—God's transcendent beauty revealed paradoxically on the Cross and man's beauty as God's work of art, to quote Ratzinger, as depicted by Michel-angelo's genius on the ceiling of the Sistine Chapel. As believers, Ratzinger once wrote, we have the capacity and the audacity to "think and view God's creative ideas with him and translate them into the visible and the audible."[30]

[28] Translated into English by Nicholas Bethell (London: Stenvalley Press, 1973), 11–15.

[29] Ratzinger pointed out in a provocative essay on the paradoxical "aesthet-ics" of faith that: "Usually people forget to mention, however, that by redeem-ing beauty Dostoyevsky means Christ." As the context makes clear, Ratzinger means Christ Crucified *and* Risen, the two "faces" of Christ, which give rise to the paradox of the aesthetics of faith; cf. his article: "Wounded by the Arrow of Beauty" in Ratzinger, *On the Way to Jesus Christ*, trans. by Michael J. Miller (San Francisco: Ignatius Press, 2005), 41; see Mark Dooley, "Benedict XVI: Beauty as a Door to the Sacred", in Dualta Roughneen, ed., *The Best of Bene-dict: An Irish Perspective* (Cork: One by One Press, 2020), 71–76.

[30] Ratzinger, "Liturgie und Kirchenmusik", *Communio*, 15, no. 3 (1986): 106. In a sense, this echoes Ratzinger's understanding of revelation as a process that involves the active contribution of those to whom God reveals Himself.

Whereas the second and third criterion are intrinsically related to the first and overarching aim of the council, the final criterion could be said to be the litmus test of a reformed liturgy, namely, that it should result in imparting "an ever-increasing vigor to the Christian life of the faithful" (*SC* 1).

Lest anyone be led astray by nostalgia for the pre-Vatican II liturgy, the then-Cardinal Ratzinger reminded the participants at the Fontgombault Liturgical Conference in July 2001[31] how much the traditional liturgy before the council was in urgent need of reform. That, to put it mildly, the reform was not exactly what the council had intended is what motived Ratzinger to devote so much time to promoting what has been called the "reform of the reform". In the meantime, this so-called Benedictine Reform seems to have lost some of its initial steam. But it is unstoppable, since it is so desperately needed.

Divine Liturgy in the Mission of the Church

Liturgy's role in the Church's mission is sketched in the first topic treated by the Constitution on the Liturgy under the subtitle, "The Nature of the Sacred Liturgy and Its Importance in the Church's Life" (*SC* 5–13). For Ratzinger, the liturgy and the sacraments are two complementary dimensions of those acts of the Church where we encounter Christ and are transformed by Him. They constitute the Church. At the core of the sacramental system is the Eucharist, "the source and summit of the Christian life" (*Lumen Gentium* 11).

---

[31] Fontgombault Abbey, founded in 1091, destroyed during the French Revolution and reopened as a Benedictine Abbey in 1948, is renowned for its cultivation of the Latin liturgy—and today it has some one hundred monks.

The trouble is that the very notion of sacrament is no longer always clear to many today. Very often, the most one
can assume is, at best, a superficial grasp of the traditional
formulae of the manuals, such as "signs that effect that
which they signify", *ex opero operato*. Such formulae articu-
late profound truths but seem to mean little to our contemporaries, even to the theologically literate. More seriously,
the role of the sacraments (in particular, the sacraments of
initiation) in the mission of the Church to redeem mankind
is no longer clear, since the understanding of mission has
to a great extent been reduced to promoting dialogue with
representatives of the non-Christian religions, while the
notion of redemption has been transmogrified into various
forms of human liberation, action for justice, peace, and the
integrity of creation.[32] Evidently, such misunderstandings
cannot but affect the liturgy, namely, the way the sacraments are celebrated.[33] These are vast topics that cannot be
treated here except in passing.

The key to the conciliar theology of sacraments—and
so of the liturgy—is its Christology, which, in continuity

[32] It hardly needs to be mentioned that these concerns are an integral part of
the mission of the Church, but they are consequences of evangelization, not
a substitute for it. In 1970, Mary Douglas warned of the long-term tendency
in the patterns of religious behavior that accrues from the move away from
ritualism: "First, there is the contempt of external ritual forms; second, there
is the private internalizing of religious experience; third, there is the move to
humanist philanthropy. When the third stage is under way, the symbolic life of
the spirit is finished. For each of these stages social determinants can be identified" (Douglas, *Natural Symbols*, 18).

[33] By way of contrast, speaking about the sacramental nature of the New
Testament priesthood, Ratzinger states: "Sacrament means: I give what I
myself cannot give; I do something that is not my work; I am on a mission and
have become the bearer of that which another has committed to my charge"
(*Called to Communion: Understanding the Church Today*, trans. Adrian Walker
[San Francisco: Ignatius Press, 1996], 115; cf. also 68). At the core of the mission
is, of course, forgiveness of sins (cf. also ibid., 64–65; 147–52).

with the whole of tradition, confesses that Christ's humanity united with the person of the Word "was the instrument of our salvation" (*SC* 5). The sacraments are rooted
in (and shaped by) the humanity of Christ, and they are
made efficacious by his divinity. Ratzinger devoted the
Salzburg Hochschulwocke lectures in 1965 to the topic:
The Sacramental Foundation of Christian Existence. There he
recovers the existential and ritual origins of the sacrament
in the rites common to world religions, which in turn
express the human way of coping with, and responding
to, those primordial human, bodily experiences such as
birth and death, that is, by means of rituals common to
mankind though particular in locality. Those rituals common to mankind were in the course of salvation history
shaped by the initiative of God, who reaches out to man
to enable him to enter into union with God in the specific history of the chosen people that began with Abraham and culminated in the Incarnation. The Christian
sacraments, prepared for through the experience of Israel,
originated in the historical Jesus of Nazareth; they receive
their transformative power from his death and Resurrection made present now through the Holy Spirit. In the
course of the Church's history, the Church's complex
liturgical rites were developed with man's own deepening
understanding (and his creativity in response to the Spirit's
promptings) under the direction of the apostolic authority
(both local and universal). We will return to this theme
in detail later. For the moment, it suffices to say that,
for the Council Fathers, the sacraments are central to the
apostolic mission of the Church. That mission is not only
to *preach* the Gospel of salvation to every creature (repentance, liberation from sin, and union with God), but to
enable mankind to *share* in the salvation he won for us on
the Cross, namely, His own divine life—what the Fathers

called *theōsis* (divinization)[34]—by means of the faith-filled
celebration of sacraments. Reborn in Christ, we join in
the cosmic liturgy embracing heaven and earth, which
is the final goal of God's creation.[35]

?• ?• ?•

These are some of the themes to be treated in this short
exploration of the inner dynamics of the liturgy inspired
by Joseph Ratzinger's theology.[36] In chapter 1, the
"word"-character of the liturgy which is specific to the

[34] This is often seen as a characteristic of Orthodox theology, but it is none-
theless central to the Catholic tradition; see *Called to Be Children of God: The
Catholic Theology of Human Deification*, ed. David Vincent Meconi, S.J., and Carl
E. Olson, with a foreword by Scott Hahn (San Francisco: Ignatius Press, 2016);
for a succinct account, see Billy Swan, *Love Has a Source* (Maynooth-London:
St. Paul's Publishing, 2020), 21–28.

[35] See Ratzinger, *'In the Beginning . . .' A Catholic Understanding of the Story
of Creation and the Fall*, trans. Boniface Ramsey, O.P. (Grand Rapids, Mich.:
Eerdmans, 1995), 27–39; Joseph Ratzinger/Benedikt XVI. *Gottes Projekt:
Nachdenken über Schöpfung und Kirche*, with a foreword by Egon Kapellari, ed.
Michael Langer and Karl-Heinz Kronawetter, together with Georg Schmutter-
mayr (Regensburg: Verlag Friedrich Pustet, 2009), 40–47.

[36] On his theology of liturgy, see: *Eucharistie Mitte der Kirche: Vier Predigen*
(Munich: Erich Wewel Verlag, 1978); *The Feast of Faith: Approaches to a Theology of the Liturgy* (San Francisco: Ignatius Press, 1986); *A New Song for the Lord:
Faith in Christ and Liturgy Today* (New York: Crossroads, 1996); but above
all: *The Spirit of the Liturgy*, trans. John Saward (San Francisco: Ignatius Press,
2000). See also the collections of articles edited by Stephan Otto Horn and
Vinzenz Pfnür in J. Ratzinger, *God Is Near Us: The Eucharist at the Heart of Life*,
trans. Henry Taylor (San Francisco: Ignatius Press, 2003); John F. Thornton
and Susan B. Varenne, eds., *The Essential Pope Benedict XVI: His Central Writings
and Speeches* (San Francisco: Harper, 2007), 141–210. Many of his writings on
liturgy are reprinted in Joseph Ratzinger, *Theology of the Liturgy: The Sacramental
Foundation of Christian Existence*, ed. Michael J. Miller, trans John Saward, Kenneth Baker, S.J., Henry Taylor, et al., vol. 11 of Joseph Ratzinger, Collected
Works (San Francisco: Ignatius Press, 2014) [634 pages, including index]. For
an account of the main contours of his theology, see Joseph Murphy, *Christ Our
Joy: The Theological Vision of Pope Benedict XVI* (San Francisco: Ignatius Press,

Judeo-Christian tradition is examined. It is a defining, indeed, *the* defining, characteristic of the Christian sacraments. One of the main objectives of the reform of the liturgy as intended by Vatican II was the much-discussed notion of *participatio actuosa*—the promotion of greater participation on the part of the ministers and faithful alike, a concern that was first articulated by Pope Saint Pius X. It seems to me that what is meant by this potentially misleading conciliar aim can best be gleaned from Ratzinger's eucharistic theology of creation and covenant. These themes are teased out in chapter 2 on cosmic worship. As mentioned already, beauty (aesthetics) is of the essence of liturgy, so that in chapter 3, attention is paid to Ratzinger's theology of the sacral nature of art and architecture—creating that sacred space where heaven touches earth, which is demanded by our very humanity now transformed into Christ's Body. In chapter 4, the kind of music suited to liturgical celebration is explored by engaging in a criticism of the dominant theory of Church music after the council that was originally proposed by Karl Rahner

2008); Tracey Rowland, *Ratzinger's Faith: The Theology of Pope Benedict XVI* (Oxford and New York: Oxford University Press, 2008); Rowland, *Benedict XVI: A Guide for the Perplexed* (London and New York: T&T Clark, 2010); Scott W. Hahn, *Covenant and Communion: The Biblical Theology of Pope Benedict XVI* (Grand Rapids, Mich.: Brazos Press, 2008); Emery de Gaál, *The Theology of Pope Benedict XVI* (Basingstoke: Palgrave Macmillan, 2013); De Gaál, *O Lord, I Seek Your Countenance: Explorations and Discoveries in Pope Benedict XVI's Theology* (Steubenville, Ohio: Emmaus Academic, 2018); Kurt Koch, *Das Geheimnis des Senfkorns: Gründzüge des theologischen Denkens von Papst Benedikt XVI*, Ratzinger Studien, vol. 3 (Regensburg: Verlag Friedrich Pustet, 2010); Siegfried Wiedenhofer, *Die Theologie Joseph Ratzingers/Benedikt XVI: Ein Blick auf das Ganze* (Regensburg: Verlag Friedrich Pustet, 2016). Of particular interest, due to the way they reflect the early stage of his theology, are two talks he gave to the Österreichische Theologenwoche, July 14–20, 1958, now published for the first time under the title: "Kirche und Liturgie (1958)", *Mitteilungen des Institut Benedikt XVI*, 1 (2008): 13–27.

and Hubert Vorgrimler. Ritual—the human dynamics of
the liturgy—is a theme that runs through the whole book
but is explored most fully in chapter 5 in connection with
the Sacrifice of the Mass on the basis of the findings of eth-
nology with regard to the universal nature of primordial
rituals. An excursus applies these insights to the proposal
of the Synod of Bishops on the Pan-Amazon Region to
create an Amazonian Rite. Here, attention is paid to the
council's second criterion for renewal: adapting the liturgy
"to the needs of our age" as expressed in diverse cultural
contexts. Finally, chapter 6, entitled "A New Liturgy for a
New Epoch", is an attempt by way of conclusion to situate
the "reform of the reform" within the broader horizon of
the mission of the postconciliar Church, and more specifically, within the salvific-historical setting of the beginning
of the third millennium. Though the text of this book was
completed before the publication of Pope Francis' motu
proprio (a papal legislative act arising from the initiative of
the pope): *Traditionis Custodes*, I hope that what follows,
but in particular the final chapter, might contribute to a
more balanced discussion of some of the issues raised by
the pope.

Chapter One

WORSHIP AND WORD

*When viewed in the light of the mystery of the heavenly liturgy,
our festive celebrations make two demands on us. The first
demand is for faith and conversion, because a celebration is a
moment of intensity in the coming of the Lord.... The second
demand has to do with the authenticity of our lives. How can we
be filled with jubilant wonder and thanksgiving in our celebrations
... if the power of the Resurrection does not daily penetrate the
depths of our sinfulness and death?*

—Jean Corbon

In his introduction to his collected writings on the liturgy,
Pope Benedict XVI explains why he decided that the volume on the liturgy should be the first to be published in
the series of some sixteen volumes of his Collected Works
(published by the *Institut Papst Benedikt XVI*, Regensburg,
and in English translation by Ignatius Press, San Francisco)
as volume 11, encompassing, in the English translation, 634
pages of text.[1] He recalls how, more or less by accident,

[1] See Pope Benedict XVI's statement explaining why he chose the topic
of liturgy: "On the Inaugural Volume of My Collected Works", in Joseph
Ratzinger, Collected Works, hereafter abbreviated *JRCW*, vol. 11, ed. Michael
J. Miller; trans. John Saward, Kenneth Baker, S.J., Henry Taylor, et al. (San
Francisco: Ignatius Press, 2014): xv–xviii. In connection with the following
comments, see also Ratzinger, *Theological Highlights of Vatican II*, introduction
by Thomas P. Rausch, S.J. (1966; New York and Mahwah, N.J.: Paulist Press/
Deus Books, 2009), 31.

the Second Vatican Council began its task of enabling
Christianity to engage more effectively with a changed
world by first tackling the topic of the divine liturgy. The
council could do so, he comments, since the document on
the liturgy was the least controversial of all the preparatory
texts. It also enabled the Council Fathers to gain the conciliar expertise needed to tackle other, more controversial,
documents. But, Pope Benedict notes, what appeared to
be an accident was in fact of great significance with regard
to the council's true order of preference. By giving their
attention first to the theme of liturgy, the Council Fathers
highlighted in no uncertain terms the primacy of God.

God first: that is the true significance of the decision of
the Council Fathers to devote their attention to the divine
liturgy.[2] When God is no longer the focus of our attention, everything else gets out of focus. The pope quotes the
Rule of Saint Benedict: "Nothing is to be preferred to
the liturgy", and he applies this monastic dictum to the life
of the Church as a whole as well as to each one person-
ally. He also recalled the etymology of the term "orthodoxy", the second half of which comes from the Greek
word δόξα, meaning, not just opinion, but glory, as found
in the term *doxology*. Orthodoxy is not only the right *opinion* about God, but is, first and foremost, the right way to
glorify God, to respond to Him. For that is the fundamental
question posed by anyone who begins to come to terms
with himself: How should I encounter God? Learning the
right way to adore—orthodoxy—that, above all, is what
we receive from the faith.

---

[2] "God first" is also the *cantus firmus* of Ratzinger's entire oeuvre. "And only
where God rules, only where God is acknowledged in the world, is man also
held in honor; only there can the world be set right. The primacy of worship
is the fundamental prerequisite for the redemption of mankind" (Ratzinger, *On
the Way to Jesus Christ*, trans. Michael J. Miller [San Francisco: Ignatius Press,
2005], 99).

The Constitution on the Liturgy was the least controversial of all the documents during its passage through the council. As Ratzinger and others have commented, it was the mature fruit of the earlier Liturgical Movement that spanned over half a century or more before the council was assembled. The Council Fathers did not foresee that the reforms it initiated would cause such turbulence. Nor did they expect a controversy that would, in effect, end in schism. The objective of the preconciliar Liturgical Movement, Ratzinger pointed out, was to overcome the reductionism of the Neoscholastic sacramental theology that had been sundered from its actual realization in liturgical form.[3] That theology had reduced the sacrament of the altar to its constituents of matter and form: bread and wine being the matter, the words of institution the form; only these are necessary, everything else can be changed.[4] On this point, Ratzinger comments rather pointedly, both traditionalists and modernists could shake hands with each other. The object of the earlier liturgical reform had been to overcome such reductionism and help us understand liturgy as the rich, complex product of a living organic tradition, whose inner form had been shaped, and so had matured, over time.[5] For this reason, it cannot be hacked into pieces but must be seen and lived in its authentic

[3] See Tracey Rowland, *Ratzinger's Faith: The Theology of Pope Benedict XVI* (Oxford and New York: Oxford University Press, 2008), chap. 7, esp. 125–26.

[4] *JRCW* 11:591–92; see also 559–60.

[5] Reflecting on his experience as a child of entering the world of the liturgy (entwined, as it were, in the everyday life of the village with all its human drama), Ratzinger recalled that: "It was becoming more and more clear to me that here I was encountering a reality that no one had simply thought up, a reality that no official authority or great individual had created. This mysterious fabric of texts and actions had grown from the faith of the Church over the centuries. It bore the whole weight of history within itself, and yet, at the same time, it was much more than the product of human history" (*Milestones: Memoirs, 1927–1977*, trans. Erasmo Leiva-Merikakis [San Francisco: Ignatius Press, 1998], 20).

wholeness. "Anyone like myself, who was moved by this perception in the time of the liturgical movement on the eve of the Second Vatican Council, can only stand, deeply sorrowing, before the ruins of the very things they were concerned for."[6]

A second general comment by Pope Benedict XVI is related to this. Liturgy is the communal nature of worship: the habitat of the sacraments, the oxygen they need to breathe. Liturgy is something living, a communal expression of our human response to Christ's offer of grace that we call sacrament. But what is a sacrament?

Sacraments are liturgical acts of the Church in which the Church is involved as Church, that is, in which she not only functions as an association but takes action on the basis of that which she herself has not made and in which she gives more than she herself can give: the inclusion of man in the gift that she herself receives. This means that in the sacrament, the entire continuum of history is present—past, present, and future. As *memoria*, it must reach down into the roots of universal human history and thus meet man in his present moment and give him a *praesens*, a presence of salvation, whose essence is that it opens up a future extending beyond death.[7]

---

[6] Joseph Cardinal Ratzinger, review of Alcuin Reid, O.S.B., *The Organic Development of the Liturgy*, in *Adoremus*, vol. 10, no. 8 (November 2004): adoremus .org/2004/11/the-organic-development-of-the-liturgy/. Indeed, in his essay (originally published in 1973), "Ten Years after the Beginning of the Council—Where Do We Stand?" (*Dogma and Preaching: Applying Christian Doctrine to Daily Life*, ed. Michael J. Miller; trans. Michael J. Miller and Matthew J. O'Connell [San Francisco: Ignatius Press, 2011], 377–84), in which he analyzes the cultural and related theological causes of the crisis that followed the council that, among other things, resulted in the radical dismantling of the liturgy; this is essential reading for anyone who wants to understand the present situation (see chapter 6 below).

[7] *JRCW* 11:184.

In his concluding comments at the conference held in the Benedictine Abbey of Fontgombault (July 24, 2001), the then-Cardinal Ratzinger called on his audience to rediscover the truth that liturgy is not simply a complex of ceremonies aimed at giving the transubstantiation of the species a certain permanence and ceremony.[8] It is, rather, the world of the sacrament as such. Accordingly, liturgy presupposes a proper understanding of what is meant by sacrament. It is Ratzinger's unique sacramental theology, it seems to me, that lies at the heart of all his many writings on liturgy. Reflecting on these writings in his introduction to his collected works on the liturgy, he informs us as to why he first gave his attention to liturgy. Fundamental theology was the initial choice he made as his chosen theological discipline, because, as he confesses, he wanted to get to the root of the question: Why do we believe? Implicit in that question is another question, namely, what is the right answer we must give to God, which evidently includes the question as to the true nature of worship. "I was concerned, not about the specific problems of liturgical studies", he admits, "but always about anchoring the liturgy in the foundational act of our faith and, thus, also about its place in the whole of our human existence."[9]

ૐ ૐ ૐ

---

[8] Describing certain textbooks of theology in use before Vatican II, Ratzinger wrote that: "Eucharistic theology had been reduced to an ontological and juridical problem, everything else being considered as beautiful ceremonies, interesting, and which might or might not be capable of interpretation in an allegorical sense, but not as the reality in which the Eucharist has its concrete existence" (Ratzinger, "Assessment and Future Prospects", in Alcuin Reid, O.S.B., ed., *Looking Again at the Question of the Liturgy with Cardinal Ratzinger: Proceedings of the July 2001 Fontgombault Liturgical Conference* (Farnborough: Saint Michael's Abbey Press, 2003), 146 [*JRCW* 11:559].

[9] *JRCW* 11:xvi.

Though Ratzinger lectured on the sacraments in Regensburg, he never got an opportunity to write a full-blown
sacramental theology. This is to be found in fragments
scattered throughout his volume on the liturgy in his
Collected Works. That volume includes two remarkable
papers devoted expressly to sacramental theology, one at
the Salzburg *Hochschulwochen* in 1965,[10] already mentioned
above, and the other in 1978 at the Catholic University of
Eichstätt.[11] In his Collected Works on the liturgy, he has
placed them in a section of their own (section B), immediately after his key publication: *The Spirit of the Liturgy*,
under the title: "Typos—Mysterium—Sacramentum". Let
us examine this more closely.

In the introduction to his Collected Works on liturgy,
the pope stresses that the aim of all his earlier writings on
this subject was to get beyond the often-petty questions
about this or that form so as to situate liturgy in its wider
context.[12] This he achieved by working out the implications of three fundamental principles (themes)[13] for
understanding Christian liturgy. In the first instance, we
have the inner relationship between the Old and the New
Testaments.[14] If one fails to see the intrinsic connection

[10] Ratzinger, "The Sacramental Foundation of Christian Existence", an
excerpt made by the author of his four-hour-long lecture given to the Salzburg
Hochschulwochen in 1965; Ratzinger, "On the Concept of Sacrament", a public
lecture to the University of Eichstätt given at the invitation of the university's
Catholic Theological Faculty on January 23, 1978. Both are to be found in
JRCW 11:153–84.

[11] *JRCW* 11:169–84.

[12] See in particular Emery de Gaál, *The Theology of Pope Benedict XVI: The
Christocentric Shift* (New York: Palgrave Macmillan, 2010).

[13] Ratzinger uses the loose term *Kreise* (circles), which I have translated as
"principles", which, admittedly, does not do justice to the notion of a cluster
of themes implied in the term "Kreis".

[14] See Joseph Cardinal Ratzinger/Pope Benedict XVI, *God's Word: Scripture—
Tradition—Office*, ed. Peter Hünermann and Thomas Söding, trans. Henry Taylor

of Christian worship with the heritage of the Old Testament, Ratzinger claims, the liturgy simply cannot be
understood. This is the most basic of all three principles
and is summed up in the title: "Typos—Mysterium—
Sacramentum". To be more precise, Ratzinger shows
why the Christian notion of sacrament can only be understood when the Old Testament is interpreted first of all
typologically, that is, seeing its events, words, and rites as
representing types of Christ (as anticipating Him), who
fulfilled them (cf. 1 Cor 10:11). Related to this is the central Greek term *mysterion*. For Saint Paul, the term refers
to God's secret design for mankind that He had prepared
from the beginning: God's primordial purpose in creation,
which is to unite man with God and so to unite all things
in Christ (cf. Eph 1:9–10). In the course of the centuries,
the Greek term *mysterion*, translated into Latin as *sacramentum* (a sacred oath), would come to mean sacrament as we
understand it today.

Another principle is the cosmic character of the liturgy.[15]
The liturgy, Ratzinger insists, celebrates the breadth, and
reaches into the depth, of the cosmos, encompassing at
the same time creation and history. This, for example,
was the intent behind the ancient orientation of prayer,
namely, prayer facing the rising sun: it signifies "that the
Redeemer to whom we pray is also the Creator and, thus,

(San Francisco: Ignatius Press, 2008), in particular 91–126; see also De Gaál,
Theology of Pope Benedict XVI, 111–17; Scott W. Hahn, *Covenant and Commu-
nion: The Biblical Theology of Pope Benedict XVI* (Grand Rapids, Mich.: Brazos
Press, 2009), esp. 91–113.

[15] See Hahn, *Covenant and Communion*, 163–85; Ratzinger, *"In the Beginning
..." A Catholic Understanding of the Story of Creation and the Fall*, trans. Boniface
Ramsey, O.P. (Grand Rapids, Mich.: Eerdmans, 1995); see also Uwe Michael
Lang, "Benedict XVI and Church Architecture", in D. Vincent Twomey,
S.V.D., and Janet E. Rutherford, eds., *Benedict XVI and Beauty in Sacred Art and
Architecture* (Dublin: Four Courts Press, 2011), 116–19.

that the liturgy always contains a love for creation and the responsibility for it".[16]

More *ad rem* is perhaps the third theme, namely, world religions.[17] Ratzinger's original interest, we saw, was "about anchoring the liturgy in the foundational act of our faith and, thus, with its place in the whole of our human existence".[18] While lecturing on the theology of the sacraments in the Major Seminary of Papua New Guinea and the Solomon Islands in Bomana, near the capital Port Moresby, I first paid attention to the aboriginal rites and myths that gave cohesion and meaning to the numerous indigenous tribes in that vast country so that they (and the members of the tribes) could survive and flourish for thousands of years. They—or rites of a similar kind—are at the root of the rituals of all the world religions. I wondered at what possible connection they might have with the Christian rites. So did my students, many of whom had taken part in various rites of initiation. Looking for help, I turned to the work of the anthropologists of ritual.

---

[16] *JRCW* 11:vii; see Erik Peterson, "Das Kreuz und das Gebet nach Osten", in *Frühkirche, Judentum und Gnosis* (Rome: Herder, 1959), 15–35. Peterson recovered the original significance of public worship *ad orientem*, which, according to F.J. Dölger, can be dated back to ca. A.D. 100, if not earlier (cf. 29); Peterson also demonstrates that the cross in the apse of early churches did not depict the crucifixion, but, arising from the very nature of Christian worship, was an eschatological sign, a symbol of His Judgment and His Victory (cf. 32). See Uwe Michael Lang, *Turning towards the Lord*, 2nd ed., with an introduction by Joseph Ratzinger/Pope Benedict XVI (San Francisco: Ignatius Press, 2009); Stephan Heid, *Altar und Kirche. Prinzipien christlicher Liturgie*, 2nd ed. (Regensburg: Schnell & Steiner, 2019), 233, 244–349, 380; cf. also Heid, "The Altar as Centre of Prayer and Priesthood in the Early Church", in Mariusz Biliniewicz, ed., "Agere in persona Christ: *Aspects of the Ministerial Priesthood. Proceedings of the Seventh Fota International Conference, 2014* (Wells, Somerset: Smenos, 2015), 27–53.

[17] Ratzinger's comprehensive theology of the world religions is to be found especially in his book *Truth and Tolerance: Christian Belief and World Religions*, trans. Henry Taylor (San Francisco: Ignatius Press, 2004).

[18] *JRCW* 11:vi.

But it was Ratzinger who provided me with the key both to interpreting the aboriginal rituals and to making the connection with liturgy as the celebration of the sacraments. Certain moments in human life—birth and death, meals and marriage—touch us so deeply that they dispose our souls to what transcends the mundane. (I will return to this in chapter 5.) The anthropologist Victor Turner discovered in his fieldwork in Africa that such aboriginal rites both express and have their source in these primal human experiences. Turner coined the term "liminal"[19] to describe the effect on the participants in such ritual celebrations.

These liminal moments, Ratzinger stresses (though he does not use the term as such), are related to *bios*, i.e., to physical life, which for man is always shot through with spirit, with meaning. He illustrates this by examining the universal experience of meals, which, properly understood, involve more than physical nourishment—they create community, fellowship, not only horizontally, with our fellows, but with God, the Giver of all. In another context, he recalls how, in all world religions, sacrifice, the core of worship, invariably involves a meal, communion with the Divinity and with those participating in the offering of the sacrifice. In a word, in the world of ritual, there is no opposition between meal and sacrifice, as contemporary liturgists tend to claim. Ratzinger recalls Bonaventure's insight into what the mediaeval theologians called the sacraments of creation, namely, marriage and repentance. The nature of marriage as a natural sacrament rooted in *bios* is obvious. And though repentance is a specifically spiritual experience, it expresses itself bodily in tears and craves absolution, as evidenced in the many ritual washings and purifications

---

[19] From the Latin, *limen* = threshold or the "in-between"; see Victor W. Turner, *The Ritual Process: Structure and Anti-Structure* (New York: Aldine Publishing, 1969), especially, chapter 3: "Liminality and Communitas", 94–130.

that are to be found in all religions; these, in turn, were incorporated into the Old Testament rites, including that of the scapegoat. And finally, there are the primordial social sacraments, kingship and priesthood, which expressed, as it were, the transcendent dimension of society: what unites past, present, and future and so gives society its inner coherence. It is a profoundly significant characteristic of the New Testament, indeed, its distinctive character vis-à-vis all other religions, that the sacral nature of kingship was *not* recognized: political authority is essentially a profane activity.[20] It is worth noting in passing that Ratzinger's theology of political life elaborates on the negative implications for the contemporary world of this radical break with the religious traditions of mankind.[21]

In the Old Testament, we find that these primordial cultic actions or rites that are common to all the world religions—such as the offering of firstfruits—have been

[20] See also Joseph Ratzinger/Pope Benedict XVI, *Church, Ecumenism, and Politics: New Endeavors in Ecclesiology*, trans. Michael J. Miller et al. (San Francisco: Ignatius Press, 2008), 155–57; 203–4. There is, of course, no denying that, in the course of the Church's history, attempts were made to turn political authority into a sacral entity, expressed above all in the coronation ceremonies of Byzantium and the Holy Roman Empire. The last survivor of these elaborate ceremonies is probably the magnificent coronation rite of the English monarch, last used for the coronation of Queen Elizabeth II in 1952. With regard to the perennial temptation to sacralize political power (beginning with Constantine), see D. Vincent Twomey, S.V.D., "Reverberations of the Great Persecution on Church-State Relations in the East and West", in the *Proceedings of the Fifth Patristic Conference* (Dublin, 2008); see also Joseph Ratzinger/Pope Benedict XVI, who, commenting on the third temptation of Jesus, described this as the perennial temptation of the Church in history: *Jesus of Nazareth: From the Baptism in the Jordan to the Transfiguration* (New York: Doubleday, 2007), 39–40.

[21] See, above all, Joseph Cardinal Ratzinger, *Church, Ecumenism, and Politics*, especially 193–208; see also Rowland, *Ratzinger's Faith*, 105–22; D. Vincent Twomey, S.V.D., "An Introduction to Ratzinger's Theology of Political Life", in Kenneth D. Whitehead, ed., *The Thought of Joseph Ratzinger, Pope Benedict XVI: Proceedings from the 32nd Annual Convention of the Fellowship of Catholic Scholars, Providence, Rhode Island, September 25–27, 2009* (Chicago: University of Scranton Press, 2009), 23–65.

transformed into celebratory links to (or, rather, memorials of) those historical events that shaped the chosen people in the past and that at the same time point to their future expectations of God's design for them. Those rites were shaped anew by the prophetic *word* that transformed primordial rituals into history-shaping ritual actions that not only remembered (reenacted, in a sense) past salvific events, but also opened the existential worshipping community up to the future.[22] This process eventually found expression in the Temple sacrifices, i.e., up to the destruction of the Temple at the time of the Babylonian captivity. In exile, the prophets discovered a new form of sacrifice to make up for the absence of the Temple worship—namely, a contrite and broken heart (cf. Ps 51 [50]). And with this more spiritual kind of sacrifice grew the hope for the restoration of the Temple in Jerusalem.

Since none of the subsequent stone buildings could satisfy that hope, the way was left open for the expectation of a new Temple, an expectation that in the consciousness of the early Christians was realized in the Church, the Body of Christ, at the core of which is the Paschal Mystery, the source of all the sacraments. The postexilic discovery of worship-in-the-spirit encountered a similar movement in Greek thought: the Greek thinkers literally saw through their own inherited myths and rites to discover the eternal *Logos*. Evidence of this growing convergence of Hebrew

[22] Here Ratzinger is applying the findings of Thierry Maertens, *Heidnisch-jüdische Wurzeln der christlichen Feste* (Mainz: Matthias-Grüewald Verlag, 1965). "[The Jewish feasts] originate from celebrations of nature religion and thus tell of Creator and creation; they then become remembrances of God's actions in history; finally, they go on from there to become feasts of hope, which strain forward to meet the Lord who is coming, the Lord in whom God's saving action in history is fulfilled, thereby reconciling the whole of creation. We will see how these three dimensions of Jewish feasts are further deepened and refashioned as they become actually present in Jesus' life and suffering" (*Jesus of Nazareth: From the Baptism in the Jordan*, 307).

prophecy with Greek thought can be found in the Wisdom literature of the Old Testament.[23] Both strands meld into one in the New Testament, as in Saint Paul's description of the new form of worship inaugurated by the Paschal Mystery: *logikē latreia (thysia)* [literally, a word-like worship].[24] This term is found in his letter to the Romans 12:1f.[25] as "the Christian response to the cultic crisis of the whole ancient world. The sacrifice is the 'word', the word of prayer, which goes up from man to God, embodying the whole of man's existence and enabling him to become 'word' (*logos*) in himself."[26] Christian worship is, therefore, first and foremost, a life dedicated to doing God's will, the source and summit of which is what the council called "the Most Sacred Mystery of the Eucharist".[27]

---

[23] See, e.g., Thomas Finan, "Hellenistic Humanism in the Book of Wisdom", *Irish Theological Quarterly* 27 (1960): 30–48; Finan, "Hellenism and Judeo-Christian History", *Irish Theological Quarterly* 28 (1961): 83–114; reproduced in Thomas Finan, *Collected Writings*, ed. D. Vincent Twomey, S.V.D. (Dublin, 2019), 23–41 and 42–72, respectively.

[24] In Latin: *rationale obsequium*, which is echoed in the Roman Canon: "Quam oblationem tu, Deus, in omnibus, quaesumus, benedictam, adscriptam, ratam, rationabilem, acceptabilemque facere digneris ut nobis Corpus et Sanguis fiat dilectissimi Filii tui, Domini nostri Iesu Christi."

[25] The CTS New Catholic Bible translates: "Think of God's mercy, my brothers, and worship him, I beg you in a way that is worthy of thinking beings, by offering your living bodies as a holy sacrifice, truly pleasing to God."

[26] *JRCW* 11:27. For the origins of Ratzinger's notion of Christian sacrifice, see his doctoral thesis, *Volk Gottes und Haus Gottes in Augustin's Lehre von der Kirche* (St. Ottilien: EOS Verlag, 1992), where he states that "every act of Christian love, every work of mercy is in a true and authentic sense sacrifice, the realization of the sole, unique *sacrificium christianorum*" (p. 213, with reference to Saint Augustine's *City of God*, X, 6, 284). In summary: "The Church is [the Christian] people insofar as it is sacrifice" (p. 295).

[27] As Father Joseph Fessio, S.J., points out about the chapter on the Mass in *Sacrosanctum Concilium*: "It's not called 'The Eucharist' or 'The Mass'; it's called 'The Most Sacred Mystery of the Eucharist.' Even in the chapter title, you have the sense that what's important is mystery, sacredness, awe, the transcendence of God" ("The Mass of Vatican II", *Catholic World Report*, July 23, 2021).

In his programmatic address to the Liturgical Institute, Trier, in 2003, to mark the fortieth anniversary of the promulgation of Vatican II's Constitution on the Liturgy, Ratzinger stressed the sacrificial nature of Christian worship. "For the liturgy, 'through which the work of our redemption is accomplished', most of all in the divine sacrifice of the Eucharist, is the outstanding means whereby the faithful may express in their lives, and manifest to others, the mystery of Christ and the real nature of the true Church" (SC 2). Ratzinger comments: "Because the liturgy is the accomplishment of redemption, it communicates to people this redemption dynamic—from the visible to the invisible, from activity to contemplation, from the present to the future city we seek."[28] He quotes Origen: "In fact, we must go beyond everything", and in this context refers to the final temptation as expressed by Goethe's Faust: *Verweile doch, du bist so schön* [Stay, please, you are so fair]. This, Ratzinger says, shows an ultimate awareness of the need to keep alive what he calls the dynamic thrust "to go beyond" this world, a thrust intrinsic to human existence—and a central concern of the Fathers of the Church. "The liturgy—so the Council shows us—leads us into this dynamism of transcendence that Augustine in his theology of the *sursum corda* [lift up your hearts] tried again and again in his sermons to bring home to the listeners. Liturgy tears us away from the visible, the present, the comfortable—and directs us toward the future city",[29] into the heavenly Jerusalem.

What happened to this vision?

ぷ ぷ ぷ

---

[28] Here Ratzinger summarizes *SC* 2.
[29] *JRCW* 11:577.

In a word, creativity took over the reform of the liturgical, as Ratzinger commented in an interview he gave in 1977.[30] Bourgeois forms of politeness began to infiltrate the liturgy like the banal greetings at the beginning of Mass or the priest waiting until all had received Communion before he did or avoiding the imperative form of blessing: "I bless *you*", which in fact undermines the basic liturgical relationship of priest and congregation.

> In the period before the appearance of the new Missal, when the old Missal was already stigmatized as antiquated, there was a loss of awareness of "rite", that is, that there is a prescribed liturgical form and that liturgy can only be liturgy to the extent that it is beyond the manipulation of those who celebrate it. Even the official new books, which are excellent in many ways, occasionally show far too many signs of being drawn up by academics and reinforce the notion that a liturgical book can be "made" like any other book.[31]

In other words, of its very nature, the liturgy is not at our disposal; it is not even at the disposal of the celebrant. It is something objective, something that has grown out of the experience of the whole Church down through the ages. This, however, does not mean that a liturgical rite is fixed in stone. "The Missal can no more be mummified than the Church herself."[32]

As is well known, the council highlighted the notion of *participatio actuosa*—active participation—in the liturgy.

---

[30] See "Liturgie—wandelbar oder unwandelbar? Fragen an Joseph Ratzinger" (an interview with the editor of the *Internationale katholische Zeitschrift "Communio"*), in *JRCW* 11:522f.

[31] *JRCW* 11:523.

[32] *JRCW* 11:524.

Behind that notion, according to Ratzinger, is the idea that the Christian liturgy in its essence and form is a coming-to-be or realization [*Vollzug*] of community. It involves reciprocal prayers, acclamations, proclamation, and common worship. Liturgical texts are characterized by terms such as "we", "you" (singular and plural), and the whole is described as part of an *actio* ("Drama"), in which all are active in a common endeavor. This insight of the Liturgical Movement was, as it were, canonized by the council. Unfortunately, it was often interpreted in a one-sided fashion.

> Many protagonists of liturgical reform seemed to think that if we only did everything together and in a loud voice, the liturgy would automatically become attractive and effective. They forgot that the spoken words also have a *meaning*, and part of *participatio actuosa* is to carry out that meaning. They failed to notice that the *actio* consists not only or primarily in the alternation of standing, sitting, and kneeling, but in inner processes. It is these that give rise to the whole drama of the liturgy. "Let us pray"—this is an invitation to share in a movement that reaches down into our inner depths. "Lift up your hearts"—this phrase and the movement that accompanies it are, so to speak, only the "tip of the iceberg". The real action takes place in the deep places of men's hearts, which are lifted up to the heights. "Behold the Lamb of God"—here we have an invitation to a special kind of beholding, at a much deeper level than the external beholding of the Host.[33]

Learning the deeper meaning of the words and symbolic actions is central to active participation in the liturgy. And it is for this reason that catechesis is essential. Even before it

[33] *JRCW* 11:526

appeared, the 2011 revised English translation was rejected on the grounds that it is too difficult for the "average" person to understand. One Irish priest opined that it should be understandable for children below the age of twelve. Apart from the patronizing clericalism behind this contention, it could be argued that a rather superficial rationalism can be detected, the assumption, namely, that we can actually understand what the liturgy (or, indeed, the faith) is all about. But Christian liturgy celebrates mysteries that are ultimately beyond comprehension.[34] For this reason, liturgical texts should be a never-ending invitation to probe more deeply into the mysteries celebrated in the divine liturgy. To respond to this invitation, however inadequately, we need the grace of humility: docility of heart. The first attempt at rendering the Latin into English following the principles of dynamic equivalence tended to reduce the text to what could be immediately understood by all—and so fostered banality as it sought the lowest common denominator. The question that needs to be addressed today is: Does the new translation foster a more reverent or sacral approach to the celebration of the liturgy?

The challenges faced by any attempt to translate the Latin text are enormous. As Latinists point out, the syntactical differences between Latin and English are so great as to render it almost impossible for any translation to do justice to both.[35] Whatever criticism one may have of the

[34] "The discursive rationalism (one might almost say 'nominalism') that is part of our Western intellectual baggage, it seems, patterns us to think meaning is the unique product of many words, rather than that the words are most often little more than triggers to chords and modulations of meaning embedded already in the minds of the hearers even before a word is spoken" (Aidan Kavanagh, "Relevance and Change in the Liturgy", *Worship* 45/2 [1971]: 66).

[35] See also the perceptive comments from an Anglican perspective by Janet E. Rutherford, " 'Putting Ashes on Our Heads': Anglican Reflections on the Problem of Liturgical English", *One in Christ* 45 (2011): 182–99; Rutherford,

literary quality of the new translation, or indeed its suit-
ability for singing (two very important aspects, since singing ought to be the main form of the liturgy),[36] there is no
doubting the fact that both priest and people now have to
think about and reflect on the meaning of the text. Now
that the Latin text of the Ordinary Form of the Roman
Rite that is at the basis of the new English translation has
been enriched by the inclusion of more ancient prayers
with their profound scriptural and patristic allusions, it
has become a greater challenge to all, but above all to the
celebrant, to search for the deeper meaning of the text.
In short, the text is not self-explanatory. Like Scripture,
which, incidentally, is the source of most of the texts
used in the Mass, the words of the new translation have
a depth, indeed, a richness that needs to be discovered
over and over again. The very awkwardness of the more
literal translation, though at times rather off-putting, can
be an invitation to "go beyond" the letter to the spirit of
the written word. It is to be hoped that it will promote a
more reverent or sacral approach to the celebration of the
liturgy by directing the attention of both priest and faithful
to what is beyond, to God.

That said, the basic criticism of the first English translation made by Thomas Finan[37] can also be applied to the
latest translation. Ritual or liturgical language, he argues, is
not simply that of communication (still less of conversation

"The Anglican Patrimony", in Janet E. Rutherford and James O'Brien, eds.,
*Benedict XVI and the Roman Missal, Proceedings of the Fourth International Liturgical
Conference 2011* (Dublin and New York: Four Courts Press and Scepter Pub-
lishers, 2013), 208–25.

[36] One of the most significant but generally unused innovations in the new
Roman Missal is the inclusion of chant for most of the Mass, including the
Eucharistic Prayers.

[37] Thomas Finan, "The Burning of the Books", *The Furrow* 23 (1974): 712–
23 (reprinted in Finan, *Collected Writings*, 430–40).

or commerce). It is more akin to the language of poetry. Finan recalls how Christine Mohrmann, when introducing her famous lectures on liturgical Latin, referred to "a basic distinction between language as communication and language as expression". Expression is, of course, a form of communication, but one that attempts to communicate more than is possible with simple communication. While clarity is the most important virtue of communication, it is not enough for expression. "For the distinction is the simple but basic one between *ex-pressing* and talking *about*, between the mimetic language of art and the discursive language of science, between the sign which aims somehow to re-present the object and the sign which merely points to it. The aim of the one is wholeness of evocation and totality of response, of the selectivity of denotation and precision of understanding." Communication aims at clarity, but this is insufficient for expression.

> It is in poetry and literature that we are most familiar with the use of language that aims beyond the mere clear. In other words, in the domains of deeper seeing and higher life where the expressive medium of language must carry a higher charge of significance. There is no such domain that goes deeper than liturgical action and art. "We are concerned with a transcendental contact between the praying individual and the divine being" [Mohrmann].[38]

Clarity may be demanded by science, technology, and economics, or even everyday communication, but more is demanded by the liturgy. Finan is not defending archaism as such, even though it played a part both in Classical and Christian Roman liturgical language. But Christianity did what the Classical tradition avoided: it incorporated

---

[38] Ibid., 431–32.

the language of the people. "So much so that Christian writers of Latin created a literary revolution both in their theory and in their practice. The revolution sprang from the realization that the language of the 'sublime' was not necessarily 'sublime language' in the conventional sense. This realization was simply an extension of the significance of the incarnation. The *humile* in matter and in form was or could now be instinct with the *grande*."[39] The important point here is that liturgical language may be simple, but it must still have the quality of transcending the mundane. It should be couched not only in the syntax and genius of the English language, but it must also reflect something of the sublime in its simplicity, which alone is suited to Divine Worship.[40]

In the meantime, for many older priests, long familiar with the earlier translation (and, indeed, for many of the laity, especially those with poetic sensibilities), who find the new translations difficult to accept—or even to read without stumbling at times—the act of obedience involved in submitting to the new translation is itself a kind of spiritual sacrifice that surely must be pleasing to God. And repetition has made the translation more familiar. There is also a theological reason for submitting to

---

[39] Cf., ibid., 432.

[40] The endeavor to find more appropriate liturgical language will continue unabated. The very nature of the Divine Worship demands that we cannot remain satisfied with what is inadequate. This, I suggest, cannot be done by a committee. It has to emerge from a community of native English-speakers— preferably in a monastic setting—as a life-long achievement, probably inspired by one or other member of the community with a sure poetic instinct. It will take time for such language to be tried and tested in the daily liturgy of the convent or monastery until it finds a resonance with the community. It, too, must grow slowly and organically. It must aspire to be sublime, as Finan defined the term, which is at one with the simplicity of the Gospel, and can only be introduced into general use gradually.

the approved translation. Before engaging in an exegesis of the Lord's Prayer in *Jesus of Nazareth*, Pope Benedict XVI gives a short exposé on prayer itself. He comments on Saint Benedict's formula in his Rule (19. 7): "*Mens nostra concordet voci nostrae*—our mind must be in accord with our voice"—as follows: "Normally, thought precedes word; it seeks and formulates the word. But praying the Psalms and liturgical prayer in general is exactly the other way round: The word, the voice, goes ahead of us, and our mind must adapt to it."[41] In other words, liturgical prayer has the dynamics of revelation: The incomprehensible God speaks to us, and we submit to his Word as expressed in the words of the psalms and the liturgy, and thus we seek to bring our minds into harmony with the contents of His words, His will, so that our hearts can affirm "Amen".

---

[41] Joseph Ratzinger, Pope Benedict XVI, *Jesus of Nazareth: From the Baptism in the Jordan*, 131.

Chapter Two

COSMIC LITURGY

Presiding at the Mass for the Solemnity of Saints Peter and Paul, 2008, Pope Benedict concluded his sermon with a commentary on Romans 15:16, which sums up Saint Paul's own understanding of his mission:

> [The Apostle] knows he is called "to be a *minister* of Christ Jesus to the Gentiles, in the priestly service of the Gospel of God as a priest, so that the offering of the Gentiles may be acceptable, sanctified by the Holy Spirit" (15:16). In this verse alone does Paul use the [Greek] word *hierourgein*— to administer as a priest—together with *leitourgos*—liturgy [*cultor* in the Roman Canon]: he speaks of the cosmic liturgy, in which the human world itself must become worship of God, an oblation in the Holy Spirit. When the world in all its parts has become a liturgy of God, when, in its reality, it has become adoration, then it will have reached its goal and will be safe and sound. This is the ultimate goal of St Paul's apostolic mission as well as of our own mission. The Lord calls us to this ministry. Let us pray at this time that he may help us to carry it out properly, to become true liturgists of Jesus Christ. Amen.[1]

See Mariusz Biliniewicz, *The Liturgical Vision of Pope Benedict XVI: A Theological Inquiry* (Oxford: Peter Lang, 2013), 30ff.

[1] Homily, Mass of the Solemnity of the Holy Apostles Peter and Paul, June 29, 2008; *AAS* 100 (2008): 464.

his passage sums up in a few dense lines the central concerns of the theology that Joseph Ratzinger had systematically developed over the course of his life as a theologian. While researching his doctoral dissertation on Saint Augustine's theology of the Church, he would have discovered—or, rather, his own conviction born of his own practice as a devout Catholic[2] would have been confirmed—that the liturgy, in particular the Eucharist, is at the heart of the Church: it makes the Church and is made by the Church. For the same reason, it is at the heart of theology. Apart from writing extensively on the liturgy, Ratzinger not infrequently would touch on the liturgy when treating other subjects, but above all in his treatment of the theology of creation.[3]

The first account of creation in Genesis, Ratzinger contends, has nothing to do with *how* we were created (such as is proposed by the scientific theory of evolution). Its message, rather, is to convey to the reader *why* we were created. According to Ratzinger, the cosmos has been brought into existence for one thing only: worship. More precisely, God called the cosmos into being so that man could share in God's Sabbath rest and hence experience that life is good and that creation, especially mankind, is very good. In the Old Testament, creation and covenant form a unity. In other words, God created man so that He might enter into a covenantal relationship with us, so that He might heal our infirmities and restore us to the relationship that He intended from the beginning of

[2] See J. Ratzinger, *Milestones: Memoirs, 1927–1977*, trans. Erasmo Leiva-Merikakis (San Francisco: Ignatius Press, 1998), 18–20.

[3] See, e.g., J. Ratzinger, *'In the Beginning ...' A Catholic Understanding of the Story of Creation and the Fall*, trans. Boniface Ramsey, O.P. (Grand Rapids, Mich.: Eerdmans, 1995), esp. 27–32; Ratzinger, *The Spirit of the Liturgy*, trans. John Saward (San Francisco: Ignatius Press, 2000), 24–34; 80–96.

the world: union with Him in Christ, the source o
joy which is the object of the Church's mission. "The
Synoptic Gospels explicitly portray Jesus' death on the
Cross as a cosmic and liturgical event: the sun is darkened,
the veil of the Temple is torn in two, the earth quakes, the
dead rise again. Even more important than the cosmic sign
is an act of faith: the Roman centurion—the commander
of the execution squad—in his consternation over all that
he sees taking place, acknowledges Jesus as God's Son:
'Truly, this man was the Son of God' (Mk 15:39).... At the
foot of the Cross, the Church of the Gentiles comes into
being. Through the Cross, the Lord gathers people together to form the new community of the worldwide
Church. Through the suffering Son, they recognize the
true God."[4]

As Ratzinger reminds us, Saint Paul expressed it in
another way: "the whole creation has been groaning with
labor pains together until now." Paul was acutely conscious
that "the creation itself will be set free from its bondage
to decay and obtain the glorious liberty of the children of
God" (Rom 8:21–2). This is already realized in the transformation of bread and wine—fruit of the earth and the
work of human hands—into the actual Body and Blood
of Christ, and in the further transformation of those who
receive the Sacred Species, who become one with Christ
and are made into the Body of Christ, the Church. Saint
Paul expresses it in 1 Corinthians 10:16–17 as follows: "The
cup of blessing which we bless, is it not a participation in
the blood of Christ? The bread which we break, is it not
a participation in the body of Christ? Because there is one

---

[4]Joseph Ratzinger/Pope Benedict XVI, *Jesus of Nazareth, Part Two: Holy Week: From the Entrance into Jerusalem to the Resurrection* (San Francisco: Ignatius Press, 2011), 224.

bread, we who are many are one body, for we all partake of the one bread." Further, Ratzinger once pointed out that Saint Augustine was granted a mystical experience of the true nature of that transformation when he heard the Lord's voice saying: "This is the bread of the strong; eat me. However, you will not change me into you [as is the case with ordinary bread], but I will change you into me."

I single out Ratzinger's eucharistic theology of creation and covenant because it highlights two of the central concerns of his extensive writings on liturgy, namely, (1) the cosmic dimension of the liturgy and (2) the roots of the ritual of the Mass not only in the word-liturgy of the synagogue, but also in the Temple worship now transformed in Christ.[5] In the flawed reform of the liturgy after the Second Vatican Council, both—the cosmic dimension of the liturgy as well as the way the Temple worship was taken up and transformed in the divine liturgy—were, for various reasons, practically ignored. The result is a truncated liturgy.

The loss of the cosmic dimension of the sacraments can only be grasped when we perceive how central matter—the human body itself and so the whole material universe—is to our new life in Christ. Matter has been remodeled into a new type of reality thanks to the Risen Lord, who, "complete with his body, now belongs totally to the sphere of the divine and eternal".[6] Commenting on

---

[5] See, e.g., Ratzinger, *Spirit of the Liturgy*, esp. 35–50; 53–84.

[6] Ratzinger, *Jesus of Nazareth, Part Two*, 274. "The body has a place within the divine worship of the Word made flesh, and it is expressed liturgically in a certain discipline of the body, in gestures that have developed out of the liturgy's inner demands and that make the essence of the liturgy, as it were, bodily visible" (Ratzinger, *Spirit of the Liturgy*, 176–77); see Biliniewicz, *Liturgical Vision*, 58–61; see the extensive treatment of Ratzinger on embodied faith in Mary McCaughey, *The Church as Hermeneutical Community and the Place of Embodied Faith in Joseph Ratzinger and Lewis S. Mudge* (Oxford: Peter Lang, 2015), 273–331.

Tertullian's saying that, from now on, "spirit and blood" have a place in God (cf. *De Resurrect. Mort.* 51:3), Ratzinger interprets those passages in Saint Paul's prison letters (cf. Col 1:12–23; Eph 1:3–23) "that speak of the cosmic body of Christ, indicating thereby that Christ's transformed body is also the place where men enter into communion with God and with one another and are thus able to live definitively in the fullness of indestructible life."[7]

Finally, in Ratzinger's sacramental theology and in his theology of the world religions, we find his profound appreciation of the fact, as mentioned above, that the ultimate roots of Christian liturgy are to be found in the cultic rituals of mankind, which reach back to the dawn of time. The same primordial, ritual nature of man enabled the Church in the course of the following centuries to unfold the mystery of the divine liturgy and express it in diverse rites of increasing density and richness of expression, including sacred art and music. This unfolding happened organically, subject only to the inner dynamics of the nature of the liturgy and the discipline of the Church's teaching authority. That is, until after Vatican II, when, it could be argued, contrary to the intention of the council and for the first time in history, the professional experts in liturgy (for the most part academics) began to restructure

[7] *Jesus of Nazareth, Part Two*, 274; commenting on the enthusiasm at the time that greeted the proclamation of the dogma of the Assumption of Mary, body and soul, into heaven, Ratzinger wrote: "At that time we—that is, people who were trying to live by faith and to think with the Catholic Church—were delighted that in an age that has rediscovered in a new and at times disturbingly passionate way the human body with its beauty, greatness, and dignity, the Church did not respond by condemning the body or even try to play down and blunt the edge of the rediscovery by drawing cautious distinctions. Instead, the Church responded with a hymn to the human body, with praise of the body that was bolder and more far-reaching than anything people outside the faith would have dared to say" ("The Assumption of Mary", trans. Matthew J. O'Connell, in Ratzinger, *Dogma and Preaching: Applying Christian Doctrine to Daily Life*, ed. Michael J. Miller [San Francisco: Ignatius Press, 2011], 357).

the liturgy around a committee table, or, to use one of Ratzinger's off-the-cuff phrases, *vom grünen Tisch fallen* (translated as "from the conference table").[8] The results are all too evident.

Pope Benedict's urgent concern for a true reform of the liturgy was expressed in his classic work *The Spirit of the Liturgy*, written during his holidays and any spare time he found as prefect of the Congregation for the Doctrine of the Faith. The permission he granted for the general use of what is now called "the Extraordinary Form of the Roman Rite", the pre-Vatican II Latin Mass, was an attempt on his part to underline existentially the continuity between it and the Ordinary Form of the Mass promulgated by Pope Paul VI, i.e., between the pre-Vatican II rite and the post-Vatican II rite, as well as to remind us of what true liturgical ritual involves: organic continuity. But the Pope Benedict's concern for a true reform of the liturgy is also expressed in the care and attention he himself gave to every celebration of Holy Mass according to the new rite over which he presided as pope.

𝄢 𝄢 𝄢

The cosmic dimension of the divine liturgy also includes the sphere of the invisible creation: the choirs of angels and saints, who incessantly adore the Majesty of God and into whose Praise of the Most High we are taken when we chant (as we should): *Sanctus, Sanctus, Sanctus* (Is 6:3;

---

[8] See especially Stephan Heid, ed., *Operation am lebenden Objekt*, a collection of scholarly papers read to a conference held at the Institute of the Görres Gesellschaft, Campo Santo Teutonico, Rome, from December 14–18, 2012, which details with scientific rigor the contrast between the Tridentine liturgical reforms with the unprecedented reform carried out in the wake of Vatican II, which quite literally amounted to an operation on a living organism.

Rev 4:8). Whereas the liturgical calendar regularly h
to remember and seek the intercession of the saints, angels
tend to be almost forgotten in the revised liturgy. Apart
from the Feast of the Archangels and the memorial of the
Guardian Angels, there are relatively few other remind-
ers of the presence of the angels in the Ordinary Form of
the Roman Rite—one mention in the *Confiteor*, more
numerously at the end of the Preface (leading into the *Sanctus*), and, most significantly, once in the First Eucharistic
Prayer (Roman Canon) after the Consecration (recalling
Judg 13:20).[9] The iconoclasm that profoundly marked and
marred the initial attempts to reform the liturgy "in the spirit
of Vatican II" removed the images and statues of angels
and saints that once adorned altars and sanctuaries, with
the resultant impoverishment of the liturgy. The rationalist,
didactic motif in the destruction of the images can be seen
in their replacement with banners containing short, scriptural texts. Admittedly, the iconoclasm was made easy in
many cases (but not all) by the poor artistic quality of these
images, which not infrequently tended to be somewhat
sentimental, even effeminate; in a word: kitsch. But the
ultimate reason was the blindness to the reality of the divine
liturgy as a sharing in the cosmic, celestial liturgy.[10] One of
the challenges facing the reform of the reform of the liturgy
is to inspire artists to represent not only the saints but also
the choirs of angels in a contemporary style that allows us
to glimpse something of their power, splendor, and majesty
and so enables us to participate more consciously in the
heavenly liturgy.

[9] "And when the flame went up toward heaven from the altar, the angel of
the LORD ascended in the flame of the altar."
[10] To recover this consciousness is the object of Jean Corbon's classic study
The Wellsprings of Worship, trans. Matthew J. O'Connell (San Francisco: Ignatius Press, 2005).

Chapter Three

SACRED ART AND ARCHITECTURE

We may not see how the artistic dimension has any importance beyond the rhetorically persuasive. An exclusive rationality has left no truth value to the imagination as a faculty or to art as its medium of communication. The coinage of the vocabulary itself has been devalued. We have no words which without further gloss will convey the sense of the imagination as the whole soul processing the world to meaning, and of the artefact as the patterned precipitate of that meaning.

— Thomas Finan

Aesthetics might appear to be something quite peripheral to the liturgy. But, as Antoni Gaudí, the Catalan architect of the Sagrada Familia Cathedral in Barcelona, echoing a long tradition that goes back to the ancient Greeks, once affirmed: "Beauty is the image of truth." In short, beauty and truth are intrinsically related; not only can the denial of the one lead to the denial of the other, but the absence of either undermines our very humanity.[1]

[1] On the profoundly human significance of aesthetics, see Mark Dooley, *Roger Scruton: The Philosopher on Dover Beach* (London and New York: Continuum, 2009), 69–117, especially 98f.; see also Kevin O'Reilly, *Aesthetic Perception* (Dublin, 2007); Joseph Ratzinger, "Wounded by the Arrow of Beauty: The Cross and the New 'Aesthetics' of Faith", in *On the Way to Jesus Christ*, trans. Michael J. Miller (San Francisco: Ignatius Press, 2005), 32–41.

To treat beauty as something peripheral—mere decoration—reflects the utilitarianism of our age, which, as we know, has profoundly influenced both modern Church architecture and the remodeling of older churches undertaken in the name of the liturgical reforms of the Second Vatican Council. Despite some impressive modern churches, the result has not infrequently been buildings with all the charm of a fridge.[2] Roger Scruton once commented that, for all its magnificence, Le Corbusier's chapel at Ronchamp has all the marks of modernistic architecture insofar as it turns public buildings into expressions of private originality. Modernist architecture is thus, by its very nature as modernist, corrosive of community. In general, buildings define the spatial environment of the human community and so cannot be just expressions of private genius. Modernist architecture, claims Scruton, can produce impressive monuments, but, by its own self-definition, it cannot produce a modern monumental *style* that can be shared by others, since modern architecture rejects the notion of common style or form rooted in tradition, one that could be adopted to suit all kinds of building, monumental or not. Without such an agreed style, it is impossible to create the kind of civic space where people can feel at home. Unlike other forms of art, such as music, painting, and literature, which are personal by nature (and usually demand a degree of *Bildung*, as the Germans put it),[3] architecture is public and so must have the humility

[2] See the perceptive comments of Roger Scruton, *Gentle Regrets: Thoughts from a Life* (London and New York: Continuum, 2005), 197–217, on the philosophical (i.e., basically anti-human) presuppositions of modern architecture; Scruton, "Classicism Now", in Mark Dooley, ed., *The Roger Scruton Reader* (London and New York: Continuum, 2009), 163–74.

[3] *Bildung* means, roughly, a certain degree of education and training as well as a broad cultural knowledge.

to subject personal genius to public welfare in the creation of that space where a community is made to feel at home. This is what characterizes the buildings of Brunelleschi and Michelangelo, whose buildings fitted into the already existing environment yet transformed it. Architecture must therefore also be rooted in tradition. Tradition is the indispensable humus of a true originality that can at the same time be contemporary yet lasting because it is rooted in the common experience of humanity.[4] What applies to buildings in general applies with particular force to church buildings, the church being, as Paige F. Hochschild pointed out, "visible speech".[5] The tradition of building churches can be traced back at least to the early third century (and probably earlier).[6]

In the wake of the council, the changes in the liturgy were seen primarily in functional terms and essentially as breaking with tradition. The public space needed for the execution of the new liturgy was similarly considered in utilitarian terms—leading, in some extreme cases, to the building of multi-purpose churches, churches serving also as parish halls so that Mass could be celebrated there in the morning and lectures, games, or parties in the evening. This is a tendency that predates the council, as we

[4] See note 2 above; see also Roger Scruton, "The Aesthetic Gaze", in *The Roger Scruton Reader*, 137–51; on the need to recover an appreciation of tradition, see Sohrab Ahmari, *The Unbroken Thread: Discovering the Wisdom of Tradition in an Age of Chaos* (London: Hodder & Stoughton, 2021), 85–102.

[5] See her stimulating article: "Church as Visible Speech", *Sacred Architechture*, 37 (June 2020): 27–31. See also in the same issue Jelena Bodganović's article: "The Domed Canopy in Byzantine Church Design", central to which is the unique design of Constantiople's magnificent Hagia Sophia recently turned again into a mosque.

[6] The oldest known house-church is that discovered in 1934 at Dura-Europos, a Roman border fortress on the Euphrates ca. A.D. 232–256 (cf. F. van der Meer and Christine Mohrmann, *Atlas of the Early Christian World*, trans. and ed. Mary F. Hedlund and H. H. Rowley [London: Nelson, 1966], 47).

can gather from the attempt by Joseph Ratzinger in 1958 to answer the question: "Should one still actually build churches today?" Churches as sacral buildings, it was suggested at the time, should be replaced by multi-purpose buildings. The theological justification for the latter was the claim that, since the frontier separating what is sacral from what is profane had been broken down by the crucified Christ, the creation of a separate sacral space amounted to nothing less than a relapse into pre-Christian religiosity.[7] Furthermore, the liturgy for which they were designed had itself been reduced to a minimum of ritual movement and gestures—and with the almost total exclusion of images. The effect of these anti-cultural forces has been not only an impoverishment of our communal worship but also the undermining of the worshipping community as a community,[8] with the consequent privatization of religion: à-la-carte Christianity.

Though anticipated by preconciliar church buildings under the influence of the Bauhaus movement, the ancient heresy of iconoclasm, it could be said, entered the Church to a certain degree through the way the conciliar reform

---

[7] Joseph Ratzinger, "Vom Sinn des Kirchenbaus", *Klerusblatt* [Munich] 38 [1958]: 418–20; the article was reprinted in his collection: *Dogma und Verkündigung* [Munich and Friburg: Erich Wewel Verlag, 1973], 269–74. (English translation: "On the Meaning of Church Architecture", in *Dogma and Preaching: Applying Christian Doctrine to Daily Life*, ed. Michael J. Miller [San Francisco: Ignatius Press, 2011], 233–43); a revised version is to be found in his *Gesammelte Schriften*, vol. 8/2, *Kirche: Zeichen unter den Völkern* [Freiburg: Herder, 2010], 1203–15, presumably based on a radio talk on the subject that he gave to Bavarian Radio, September 12, 1973; quotations are from the English trans.; see his comments in his essay "Ten Years after the Beginning of the Council", in *Dogma and Preaching*, 377–84, where he elaborates on this phenomenon. It would seem that the underlying assumptions by those who masterminded the reform fed into (or were influenced by?) the more dominant cultural currents that Scruton describes as essentially modernist. See chapter 6 below.

[8] See the works of Scruton in notes 2 and 4 above.

of the liturgy was executed. Many, including R.
would argue that that reform was *not* in fact fa:
the intent of the Council Fathers. The iconoclastic
controversy—the eighth-century debate about the legit-
imacy of sacred images—touched on the most profound
of theological issues.[9] It is no accident that the Orthodox
Churches consider the Second Council of Nicaea (A.D.
787), which definitively rejected iconoclasm, as *the* Orthodox Council par excellence.[10] One is reminded of what
the great German writer Heinrich Heine once said when
he stood before Antwerp Cathedral in awe of its beauty:
"The men who built these [cathedrals] had dogmas [i.e.,
eternal truths]. We have only opinions. And with opinions
one does not build cathedrals."[11]

The way the reform of the liturgy was implemented
after the Second Vatican Council, however, was not based
on dogmas. Rather, it was based on theological opinions, and not the richest of opinions, either. According to
Tracey Rowland,[12] the theology that guided the Liturgical Commission presided over by Cardinal Lercaro with
the assistance of Archbishop Annibale Bugnini as secre-
tary was a Neoscholasticism that was both a-historical and
a-cultural. It was only interested in essences: in a word, it

[9] See Christoph Schönborn. O.P., *God's Human Face: The Christ-Icon*, trans.
Lothar Krauth (San Francisco: Ignatius Press, 1994), especially 135–235; "Iconoclasm is not the breakthrough from the Old Testament into the New, but,
rather, the destruction of the Incarnation and thus a relapse into the Law, which
could permit no images because the Image had not yet appeared" (Ratzinger,
"On the Meaning of Church Architecture", 237).

[10] See Schönborn, *God's Human Face*, 199–206.

[11] As quoted in *30 Days*, June 1990: 3. Antwerp is mentioned as the cathedral, though my memory of this quotation, when I first came across it, was
that it referred to the cathedral of Strasbourg. In fact, it applies to all the great
cathedrals of Christendom.

[12] Tracey Rowland, *Ratzinger's Faith: The Theology of Pope Benedict XVI*
(Oxford and New York: Oxford University Press, 2008).

was minimalist—which demonstrates again that the same
Neoscholastic theology was strangely in harmony with
the most dominant forms of contemporary culture and its
art. The irony is that the whole thrust of the council was
to overcome that kind of theology. The tragedy is that
most of the liturgical experts who carried out their radical
reforms "in the spirit of Vatican II" seem to have shared
this same desiccated Neoscholasticism.[13]

There was another influential factor that, it seems to me,
fostered the minimalist approach to the liturgy, namely, the
legalistic mindset of the same liturgists who themselves had
been trained to observe the most intricate of rubrics, most
of which were removed by the liturgical reform.[14] The former rigorist approach to rubrics gave way to a legalistic
minimalism that was pursued with equal zeal.[15] What was
considered not to be absolutely necessary was judged to
be superfluous and, so, had to be removed. Though many
of the faithful, and even some clerics, were upset by the

[13] At the Fota conference, this point was contested by some liturgists, who
claimed that the minimalism that characterized the recent liturgical reform was
due rather to the influence of the Enlightenment. This may well be true, especially if we consider that modernism is the end product of the Enlightenment.
However, one could also argue that paradoxically, it was precisely due to their
efforts at overcoming the Enlightenment that Neoscholasticism absorbed some
of the unspoken assumptions of the Enlightenment. Responding to an earlier
draft of this talk, Professor Stephan O. Horn, S.D.S., in a letter to me, made
the following comment: "I am, however, not as critical with regard to church
building as you are. What I mean is that, in Germany, many good, new begin-
nings were made especially since the 1920s. It seems to me, of course, that
Romano Guardini theologically and practically prepared the way for a tendency towards reduction to what is essential."

[14] See chapter 5 below.

[15] The same phenomenon can be seen in the initial attempts to reform moral
theology as mandated by the Fathers of Vatican II. The legalistic rigorism of
the pre-Vatican II manuals gave way to the laxity of the dominant so-called
proportionalist schools of moral theology. Only in recent decades has there
been a return to a more classical approach to moral theory in terms of virtue.

resulting destruction of beautiful altars, communion rail, tabernacles, even statues, etc.—many of which ended up decorating lounge bars—their protests were dismissed by a display of clerical arrogance that justified itself by claiming obedience to the liturgical reforms of the council. Reforming clerics, too, often rode roughshod over the sensibilities of the faithful, even their familial sensitivities, since, at least in Ireland, many of those artifacts now deemed redundant had been donated by their struggling ancestors in the financially straightened times of the nineteenth century in the aftermath of the Great Famine (1845–1852), when about a million died and another million emigrated. It is no wonder that, as a result of such neo-clericalism (disguised as progressivism), many believers were alienated from the Church and remain so to this day.

But leaving that aside, the changes to the church building and to the liturgy also profoundly affected the worship of those who actually stayed behind and endured the new "stripping of the altars" (Eamon Duffy). More precisely, the changes also affected their image of God. Roger Scruton once commented perceptively: "Changes in the liturgy take on a momentous significance for the believer, for they are changes in his experience of God—changes, if you wish to be Feuerbachian, in God himself."[16] A poem by a Limerick poet Tim Cunningham entitled "Tabernacle"[17] illustrates this in a more colloquial fashion:

> It was bold, this house of gold,
> Its golden door on fire, alive,
> Dead centre on the high altar,

[16] *Philosopher on Dover Beach* (Manchester: Carnet, 1990), 115, quoted by Rowland, *Ratzinger's Faith*, 128.

[17] Tim Cunningham, *Kyrie* (Limerick: Revival Press, 2008), 18, reprinted with the kind permission of the author.

Regal, expecting the homage of bent
Knees. The sanctuary lamp flickered
Saying God was in.

They moved Him to a side altar.
I see their point, a changing
Liturgy for changing times,

Diluted like whiskey on the rocks,
An accessible deity discreet about
His thunderclap and lightning bolt,

A guy-next-door god
Who can share a pint
And chat about the football scores.

But some old codgers moan,
Imagine the whiz kids
Have taken over the manor;

Cobbled together
A granny-annexe-bathchair-god
To wheel out on occasion.

The profound significance of the break with the Church's two-thousand-year-old tradition is perhaps best illustrated by Otto von Simson in his classic work on the Gothic cathedrals,[18] where he speaks of the universal understanding of what a church building means—or, rather, once meant—for the Church: The church building is "mystically and liturgically an image of heaven.... The authoritative language of the dedication ritual of a church explicitly relates the vision of the Celestial City, as described in the Book of Revelation, to the building that is

---

[18] Otto von Simson, *The Gothic Cathedral: Origin of Gothic Architecture and the Medieval Concept of Order*, 3rd ed. (1956; Princeton, N.J.: Princeton Univ. Press, 1988).

to be erected."[19] According to von Simson, the images of
Christ in glory seated on a throne and surrounded by the
heavenly court as found in Romanesque churches indicate
the "anti-functionalism" of both Romanesque and Byzantine art: "The mystical experience that murals or mosaics
are to help invoke within the faithful is emphatically not of
this world; the celestial vision depicted is to make us forget
that we find ourselves in a building of stone and mortar,
since inwardly we have entered the heavenly sanctuary."[20]
Von Simson goes on to show how the Gothic architecture marvelously incarnated this vision in stone and glass
as determined by the speculations on geometry first articulated by Augustine under the influence of the Pythagore-
ans. In a different cultural context, the same vision guided
the artists who created the Baroque, which style the art
historian Kenneth Clarke[21] described as the natural reac-
tion of Catholics to the world-denying and body-denying
spirituality of the Reformation, which had also featured
some not inconsiderable iconoclasm. Common to both
the Gothic and the Baroque was their sacral nature: they
were "earthly manifestations of some higher design".[22]

Was that artistic development, for all its greatness, perhaps a false one? Ratzinger[23] shows how the church as a
sacral building evolved necessarily from the unique spiritualization of worship that characterized Christian worship,
namely, its incarnational nature. It was this incarnational
nature of Christian worship that posed difficulties for the

---

[19] Ibid., 8.
[20] Ibid., 9.
[21] Kenneth Clarke, *Civilisation: A Personal View* (London: British Broadcast-
ing Corporation and John Murray, 1969), which is the written text of a series
of television programmes given in the spring of 1969.
[22] Roger Scruton, "Aesthetic Gaze", 138.
[23] "On the Meaning of Church Architecture".

...conizing tendencies of the Church Fathers, such as that experienced by Augustine, and was only overcome by the Second Council of Nicaea (787). Church buildings themselves arose naturally and organically from the actual celebration of the Eucharist, which makes the death and Resurrection of Christ present. "This gathering, which we call Eucharist, is the heartbeat of its life. In it, the faith community remembers that central event of the Cross and Resurrection and, in remembering, receives the Presence. And for that purpose we build churches. As Christians we need a house for gathering, which by the way cannot exist without interior recollection."[24]

Ratzinger shows further how, already in New Testament times, the distinction between sacral and profane was made by Paul when he separated the domestic Agape meal from the celebration of the Eucharist (1 Cor 11). Further, the Church of the first three centuries conceived itself, not as a gathering of friends or a private club, but rather as a universal assembly (*ecclesia*) making public claims on a par with the Roman Empire. The result was that, when Christianity was eventually recognized as a public entity after Constantine, the Roman basilica was its preferred place of worship. This public space was thereby transformed into a sacral building, primarily by retaining the earlier orientation of the worshipping community to the east, eventually giving rise to the creation of the specific Christian sacral building we call church. The shape of the church building was determined by the special requirements needed to facilitate the main ecclesial actions of Eucharist, baptism, and reconciliation.[25] In doing so, the Christian

[24] Ibid., 237; the nuances of Ratzinger's use of the German language are often lost in translation.
[25] These ideas were developed more completely in Ratzinger's contribution to Walter Seidel, *Kirche aus lebendigen Steinen* (Mainz: Grünewald, 1975), 30–48,

community replicated what all religions in the history of
mankind have spontaneously done, namely, create sacred
spaces that, to quote Eliade, are recognized as "meeting
points between heaven and earth", each being "a point of
junction between earth, heaven and hell, the navel of the
earth, a meeting place of three cosmic regions."[26]

༂ལ ༂ལ ༂ལ

According to Tracey Rowland, one of the major differences
between Pope Benedict XVI and Pope Saint Paul VI is to be
found in their attitude toward beauty. For Paul VI, it seems

---

entitled "Auferbaut aus lebendigen Steinen" (a revised edition was published in
his *Ein neues Lied für den Herrn* [Freiburg: Herder, 1995], 105–23); a translation
of this contribution, " 'Built from Living Stones': The House of God and the
Christian Way of Worshipping God", appeared in *A New Song for the Lord:
Faith in Christ and Liturgy Today*, trans. Martha M. Matesich, 2nd ed. (New
York: Crossroad, 2005), 78–93, and subsequently in *JRCW* 11:371–87. See also
the other contributions to Seidel, especially those by Hans Urs von Balthasar
and Josef Pieper, on the occasion of the millennium celebrations of the Cathedral of Mainz. For a comprehensive account of the historical development, and
characteristic shape, of the church as a building focused on the "table of the
Lord" or "altar"—the terms were interchangeable for the early Church (cf. 1
Cor 10:21; Heb 13:10)—cf. Stephan Heid, *Altar und Kirche: Prinzipien christlicher
Liturgie*, 2nd ed. (Regensburg: Schnell & Steiner, 2019).
[26] Mircea Eliade, *Patterns in Comparative Religion* (London: Sheed and Ward,
1958), 375, as quoted in John Holm, ed., with John Bowker, *Sacred Place* (London and New York: Continuum, 1994), 5. *Sacred Place* deals with Buddhism,
Christianity, Hinduism, Islam, Judaism, Sikhism, Chinese, and Japanese religions. "Eliade went on to show how the architecture and symbolism of many
sacred buildings—temples, churches and mosques—echo something of the
central sacred space of a religion" (ibid.). This is well illustrated by Margaret
Visser, *The Geometry of Love: Space, Time, Mystery and Meaning in an Ordinary
Church* (London: Viking, 2001), where the author explores the richness of the
small, seventh-century church of Saint Agnes outside the city walls of Rome.
For a general overview, see the magnificently illustrated volume by Richard
Stemp, *The Secret Languages of Churches and Cathedrals: Decoding the Sacred Sym-
bolism of Christianity's Holy Buildings* (London: Duncan Baird, 2010).

...ve been mostly a matter of taste, something external to theology. For Pope Benedict XVI, it is something more humanly and theologically significant. In harmony with Saint Bonaventure's comments on God revealing Himself first in the beauty of creation, for Pope Benedict, "the liturgy is inherently linked to beauty",[27] it is an essential element of the liturgical action, like the experience of Peter, James, and John on Mount Tabor. Further, Benedict XVI is acutely aware of the necessity for reason to combine with aesthetic and intuitive sensibility, both in liturgy and art.

This approach colors Ratzinger's own reflections on liturgical music.[28] The same could be said about his approach to art and architecture, since, as Augustine held, at one with Plato, music and architecture are sisters. Ratzinger opposes the utility music once advocated by Karl Rahner and Herbert Vorgrimler, who stressed its pedagogical value, as we will see. "Ratzinger's argument is that liturgy is about worship of the Triune God: it is neither pedagogy or psychotherapy."[29] The latter are legitimate human needs, namely, catechesis or making people feel cozy, but they might be catered for elsewhere, such as in the Advent, Lenten, and May devotions which provide opportunities for instruction and emotional support appealing to our sentiments. Both of these are greatly needed but cannot be provided by the divine liturgy.

> The Church must not settle down with what is merely comfortable and serviceable at the parish level; she must arouse the voice of the cosmos and, by glorifying the Creator, elicit the glory of the cosmos itself, making it also glorious, beautiful, habitable and beloved. Next to

---

[27] Rowland, *Ratzinger's Faith*, 131.
[28] See below, chapter 4.
[29] Rowland, *Ratzinger's Faith*, 138.

the saints, the art which the Church has produced is the
only real 'apologia' for her history.... The Church must
maintain high standards; she must be a place where beauty
can be at home; she must lead the struggle for that "spiritualization" without which the world becomes the "first
circle of hell".[30]

[30] Joseph Ratzinger, *The Feast of Faith*, trans. Graham Harrison (San Francisco: Ignatius Press, 1986), 124–25; quoted in Rowland, *Ratzinger's Faith*, 133.

Chapter Four

SACRED MUSIC

Catholic ceremonies have an historical, social, artistic, and musical interest whose beauty surpasses all that any artist has ever dreamed, and which Wagner alone was ever able to come close to, in Parsifal—and that by imitation.

—Marcel Proust, *Death Comes for the Cathedrals*

Michael O'Callaghan, the music teacher at my old school, Christian Brothers College, Cork, was by far the most influential teacher I ever had. First of all, he taught us music appreciation. He trained our voices to sing in choirs (one of the most satisfactory aesthetic experiences one can have), and he taught us to play musical instruments at a time in Ireland when little attention was paid to such training. He managed to create a school orchestra with our limited talent, which morphed into the Cork Youth Orchestra, the first ever in Ireland. On visiting him after my ordination, I remember how this most gentle of all men expressed his profound sadness, not unmixed with anger, at the banality of the church music he had had to endure since the liturgical reforms were introduced after the council.[1]

---

[1] To remedy the situation, he composed a number of Masses, but, as far as I can see, they were rarely used.

His feelings were summed up by a remark once made by a retired primary school teacher, who in his youth had been a member of the Cork Pro-Cathedral Choir before Vatican II. He remembered with gratitude the beauty of the sung High Mass every Sunday that nourished his soul for the rest of the week. A daily Mass-goer to the end of his days, his one regret was that the reformed Mass no longer enabled him to experience that *sursum corda* that was once the weekly experience in the Pro-Cathedral.

In what perhaps is his foundational essay on sacred music, "On the Theological Basis of Church Music",[2] the then-Cardinal Ratzinger takes as his starting point the interpretation of the chapter on Sacred Music in the *Constitution on the Sacred Liturgy* as given in the commentary by Karl Rahner and Herbert Vorgrimler in the German edition of the council documents. Basically, the two German theologians saw music primarily as "merely an addition and ornamentation to the liturgy".[3] They interpreted the council's recommendation to cultivate the musical heritage of the Western Church with great care as though this should not necessarily be done within the framework of the liturgy. The Church's musical heritage, they opined, being "esoteric" by nature, should be limited to cathedrals—and, even there, such art music should not obstruct the normal "participation" of the people. "For Rahner and Vorgrimler, the normal musical component of the liturgy is hence not 'actual church music' but 'so-called utility music'."[4]

Ratzinger admits that a certain tension can be detected in the conciliar text, a tension that indeed reflects the tension in the various approaches to the subject at the council.

---

[2] In Joseph Cardinal Ratzinger, *The Feast of Faith*, trans. Graham Harrison (San Francisco: Ignatius Press, 1986), 97–126.

[3] Ibid., 97.

[4] Ibid., 98.

These, in turn, reflect a tension inherent in the subject itself, namely, the question of what constitutes sacral music. "During the Council, the Fathers became aware of a problem which had not arisen in such a pointed form before—the tension between the demands of art and the simplicity of the liturgy", and then he adds: "but when experts and pastors meet together, the pastoral issues predominate, with the result that the view of the whole [tends] to get out of focus."[5] What was expressed in the text of the council was an attempt to attain a difficult balance, one that, in the aftermath of the council, was easily tipped in favor of "utility music" with the consequent banishing of "actual church music" to the concert hall or the odd cathedral that still promoted the Church's tradition of sacred music. Ratzinger comments that "The years which followed witnessed the increasingly grim impoverishment which follows when beauty for its own sake is banished from the Church and all is subordinated to the principle of 'utility'."[6]

Instead of bemoaning the resultant banality and its attendant boredom, Ratzinger says that this negative development does force us to ask questions, the central one being whether the simplicity of the liturgy aimed at participation by all excludes real church music, or, does it perhaps actually demand it? In the final analysis, answers will not be found in theology as such, he says, which has always had a rather cool relationship with church music, but within the compass of Christian experience, i.e., within the compass of tradition.[7]

From the Baroque period down to our own day, church music has reflected the dominant mood of the time, such as

[5] Ibid., 99.
[6] Ibid., 100.
[7] Ibid.

the new interest in plainchant during the Romantic period with its nostalgia for the medieval period. The dominant mood of the modern period, according to Ratzinger, ultimately "goes back to a conception of activity, community and equality which no longer knows the unity-creating power of shared listening, shared wonder, the shared experience of being moved at a level deeper than words."[8]

The antithesis of the esoteric versus utility as formulated by Rahner and Vorgrimler is but a contemporary version of a problem that can be traced back to the dawn of Christianity, according to Ratzinger. He focuses on the relevant *quaestiones* of Saint Thomas Aquinas, whose greatness lies not least in the fact that his work "mirrors all the substantial elements of tradition".[9] Thomas' starting point in his treatment of the virtue of religion is that, though singing is in principle justified—it has been part of worship since Jesus and the apostles who sang in the synagogue brought it into the Church—nonetheless strong arguments can be made to limit singing very severely.

Thomas was confronted by three influential theological authorities, two of which had gained entry into the *Decretum* of Gratian and thus enjoyed the status of customary law. Jerome, who, rejecting the tendency of singers to show off their voices, took Ephesians 5:19 literally and said that they should simply sing with their hearts, not their gilded throats. And Saint Gregory the Great prohibited clerics ordained to the diaconate from being cantors, lest they be distracted from the ministry of proclamation of the Word and service to the poor. Pope Gregory was also aware of the moral danger of turning church music into a performance aimed at the admiration of the listeners.

[8] Ibid., 101.
[9] Ibid., 102

However, the most important argument came from the New Testament, where in Colossians 3:16 the faithful were encouraged to sing "spiritual songs", which exegetes interpreted to mean: God is honored more by the spirit than by the mouth.

Almost as an aside, Thomas makes the observation: "In praise of God the Church does not employ musical instruments ... lest it appear to be falling back into Jewish ways."[10] Ratzinger comments: "Instrumental music, understood as a 'judaizing element', simply disappeared from the liturgy without any discussion; the instrumental music of the Jewish Temple is dismissed as a mere concession to the hardness of heart and sensuality of the people at the time."[11] What Thomas could not have known is that by rejecting instrumental music and limiting herself to the vocal sphere, the early Church was in fact expressing her continuity with early Judaism by linking up with the practice of the synagogue and the puritanism of the Pharisees, who did not use musical instruments.[12] In addition, patristic exegesis under the influence of Platonism tended to interpret the opposition of the Law and the Gospel in terms of the Greek philosophical opposition of the sensual to the spiritual. Music, especially instrumental music, fell under the rubric of the sensual, while "the spiritual" tended more and more to be seen in terms of the word alone.

According to Ratzinger, the issues underlying the theological critique of music are basically two: the Platonizing tendency to spiritualization and the Aristotelian concept of God's immutability.

---

[10] Q 91 a 2 opp. 4, as quoted in ibid., 104.
[11] Ratzinger, *Feast of the Faith*, 104–5.
[12] Cf. ibid., 105.

The Church Fathers could not simply step out of the intellectual climate of their time, one that was dominated by Platonism, which in many ways was a treasured ally of early Christianity. Both stressed the need for spiritualization. But Platonism and Christianity differed in one essential way: in what is meant by spiritualization, a difference that arose from the implications of Christology.

> [I]n Christian terms, "spiritualization" is not simply opposition to the world of the senses, as in Platonic mysticism, but a drawing near to the Lord who "is the Spirit" (2 Cor 3:17; cf. 1 Cor 15:45). Therefore the body is included in this spiritualization: the Lord is "the Spirit" precisely in that his body does not experience corruption (Ps 15:9f. LXX = Acts 2:26) but is seized by the life-giving power of the Spirit. Christology reveals the central divergence from the Platonic teaching on spiritualization; its background is the theology of creation, whose inner unity is not destroyed but ratified by Christology.[13]

By adopting the more or less Puritan cult of the synagogue, the early Church initially gave cultic expression to her break with the cult of the Jewish Temple. However, Ratzinger also asks: To what extent was the early Church influenced nonetheless by John 2:13–22, with its promise of a new Temple in three days? We know that in the patristic era, the idea of the Temple was incorporated into theology, usually in an "allegorical" sense, and consequently in a strictly applied spiritualizing theology.[14] This trend was only reversed as a result of the iconoclastic controversy, when "the Greek Church's passion for the image led to a breakthrough in which Christianity's

---

[13] Ibid., 108.
[14] Cf. ibid., 109.

historical development ... succeeded in moving in the opposite direction: from the absence of images in the Old Testament to the glorification of God in the image."[15] Ratzinger adds, it is this fundamental decision that has been called into question in the postconciliar Church with her abandonment of images—and, parallel to that, the removal of "actual church music" in favor of "utility music". The issues at stake are deeper than we normally consider.

The second reason for the theological critique of music was put in a nutshell by Thomas Aquinas, when he wrote that "vocal worship is necessary, not for God's sake, but for the sake of the worshipper".[16] Ratzinger comments: "Here we see how much the ancient world's concept of God's absolute immutability and impassibility had entered into Christian thought through Greek philosophy, creating a barrier to any satisfactory theology, not only of church music, but of all prayer whatever."[17] Only with great difficulty has Christian theology managed to break free of these notions, though today we seem to have fallen back into the same basic error when prayer is understood as releasing subjective powers inherent in our humanity.

Ratzinger asks: What are the positive elements of tradition to be found in Thomas Aquinas that could form the basis for a theology of sacred music? The living experience of the liturgy, on the one hand, and the theology of the psalms, on the other. Moving from synagogue to the church, singing actually increased; new hymns were composed and found their way into the New Testament. That is the basic Christian experience of praise and joyous thanksgiving. Likewise, the theology of the psalms was

[15] Ibid., 109–10.

[16] Q 91 a1 resp., quoted in ibid., 112.

[17] Ratzinger, *Feast of the Faith*, 112. If God is unchanging and so cannot be moved by our prayer, why pray, why ask Him for anything?

utterly devoid of any puritanical streak. The whole wealth
and breadth of Israel's worship fed into the worship of
the early Church though the psalms. Thomas concludes
his reflections on vocal music in church by quoting Psalm
33:2–4: "his praise shall continually be in my mouth ....
Let the afflicted hear and be glad. O magnify the Lord
with me." Ratzinger comments: "By quoting from the
psalms, Thomas is in fact saying Yes to that joy which
expresses itself and in so doing unites those who participate (and this includes particularly those who 'listen'); this
expressed joy manifests itself as the presence of the glory
which is God: in responding to this glory, it actually *shares*
in it."[18] The psalms echo the heavens that proclaim the
glory of God now manifest in the crucified and risen Lord.
Ratzinger comments: " 'Glorification' is the central reason
why Christian liturgy must be cosmic liturgy, why it must
as it were orchestrate the mystery of Christ with all the
voices of creation."[19]

Other themes found in the tradition that Thomas incor-
porates include the assertion that through praise of God,
man ascends to God and is drawn from what opposes
God. "Anyone who has ever experienced the transforming
power of great liturgy, great art, great music, will know
this."[20] This comment reminds me of a letter sent to me
once by a retired parish priest in the West of Ireland who
the previous year had attended the liturgy celebrating the
end of the Year of Priests (2009–2010) in Rome: "In our
colleges of formation, rubrics and liturgy were rigid but
here in Rome, liturgy was purification: The Holy Spirit
was here.... The morning ceremony culminated with holy

[18] Ibid., 114.
[19] Ibid., 115.
[20] Ibid., 116.

Mass done with tranquil, moving pace, amid the mosaics of Saint Paul's—and music: organ, orchestra, choir. . . . Thanksgiving time had soul."

Paraphrasing Aquinas, Ratzinger says: the sound of musical praise "awakens the inner man" and refers to the discovery Augustine made during the liturgy in Ambrose's Milan, when he, the academic, was shattered to the innermost core of his being by the sheer beauty of the music.[21]

Finally, Ratzinger asks to what extent the long-established critique of music is justified. It cannot have been entirely misplaced. Taking up the theme of the kind of spiritualization that is specific to Christianity, Ratzinger shows that it consists primarily in the inner transformation of creation by bringing it into the mode of the Holy Spirit as exemplified in the crucified and risen Lord. He says,

> In this sense, the taking up of music into the liturgy must be its taking up into the Spirit, a transformation which implies both death and resurrection. That is why the Church has had to be critical of all ethnic music; it could not be allowed untransformed into the sanctuary. The cultic music of pagan religions has a different status in human existence from the music which glorifies God in creation. Through rhythm and melody themselves, pagan music often endeavors to elicit an ecstasy of the senses, but without elevating the senses into the spirit; on the contrary, it attempts to swallow up the spirit in the senses as a means of release.[22]

A similar imbalance, he notes, is found in modern popular music, where a different kind of "god" is found and a

---

[21] Ibid.; this is the topic Ratzinger develops in his essay "Wounded by the Arrow of Beauty", in his *On the Way to Jesus Christ*, trans. Michael J. Miller (San Francisco: Ignatius Press, 2005), 32–41.

[22] Ratzinger, *Feast of Faith*, 118

different kind of salvation sought: there music becomes, not a form of purification, but a drug, an anesthetic, an escape. "If music is to be the medium of worship, it needs purifying."[23]

"The whole of Church history can be seen as the struggle to achieve the proper kind of spiritualization."[24] And the fruit of that struggle—including the role played by the unenlightened puritanism of the theologians—has been the great Church music, indeed, Western music as a whole. "The work of a Palestrina or a Mozart would be unthinkable apart from this dramatic interplay in which creation becomes the instrument of the spirit, and the spirit, too, becomes organized sound in the material creation, thus attaining a height inaccessible to 'pure' spirit. Spiritualization of the senses is the true spiritualization of the spirit."[25]

It is impossible to lay down a priori criteria for this spiritualization; it is easier to say what is excluded than what is included, as evidenced by the very general guidelines given by the Second Vatican Council. Here, too, we can appreciate the concerns of the tradition of critique found in Thomas. Saint Jerome railed against turning church music into music of the theatre; "... liturgical music must be humble, for its aim is not applause but 'edification'."[26] For this reason, it is appropriate that in church the musician is heard but not seen. But what of Thomas' preference for vocal music to the exclusion of instrumental music, based as it is on his own misunderstanding? Ratzinger is reluctant to dismiss such a deeply rooted tradition as completely

[23] Ibid., 119. My own experience of the liturgical experimentation at the Holy Spirit Regional Seminary of Papua New Guinea and the Solomon Islands (1979–1981) confirms that insight of Ratzinger's; see Excursus below.

[24] Ibid.

[25] Ibid.

[26] Ibid., 120.

mistaken. The liturgy of the incarnate Word is necessarily word-orientated. Thomas, when dealing with the objection that when something is sung it is harder to understand than when it is said, replied that the hearers, nonetheless, know the reason for singing—praise of God—and that is sufficient to rouse men to worship. Ratzinger suggests that perhaps the use of an instrument creates a greater possibility of alienation from the spirit than in the case of the voice, for which reason greater consideration must be given to the process of purification, of elevation to the spirit. And it is this essential purification that "has resulted in the development of the instruments of Western music, endowing mankind with its most precious gifts."[27]

Ratzinger concludes his reflections by proposing five basic principles:

1. "Liturgy is for all",[28] that is, it must be "catholic", communicable to all without distinction. It must be "simple", which does not mean cheap. "The greatest efforts of the spirit, the greatest purification, the greatest maturity—all these are needed to produce genuine simplicity."[29]
2. "Catholicity does not mean uniformity."[30] The council singled out the cathedral for special mention,

[27] Ibid., 121.

[28] Ibid., 122.

[29] Ibid. Simplicity, here, must be understood in the sense found in the New Testament term *haplotes*: "simplicity, sincerity, purity or probity of mind and liberality (arising from simplicity and frankness of character)", according to *The Analytical Greek Lexicon*, new and rev. ed. (n.d.). It is the attitude of Mt 18:3: "unless you turn and become like children...." It is central to Ratzinger's own spirituality (cf. Twomey, "Ratzinger on Theology as a Spiritual Science", in James Keating, *Entering into the Mind of Christ: The True Nature of Theology* [Omaha, Neb.: IPF Publications, 2014], 47–70).

[30] Ratzinger, *Feast of Faith*, 123.

stressing that in that sacred space liturgy should be more ambitious in terms of solemnity and beauty of worship than what is possible in a parish church. But the parish church should cultivate its own level of art and beauty.

3. The conciliar principle of *participatio actuosa* must be understood to reach beyond external activity. Article 30 of the Constitution on the Liturgy speaks of silence as a mode of participation.[31] Ratzinger asks: "Are receptivity, perception, being moved, not 'active' things too?"[32] While not impugning congregational singing, Ratzinger comments that, in concrete terms, "there are a good number of people who can sing better 'with the heart' than 'with the mouth'; but their hearts are really stimulated to sing through the singing of those who *have* the gift of singing 'with their mouths'."[33]

4. "A Church which only makes use of 'utility' music has fallen for what is, in fact, useless."[34] She also becomes ineffectual, since her mission is far greater: namely, to be the place of "glory", the place also where mankind's cry of distress is brought to the ear of God. The Church cannot be satisfied with domestic comfort; her task is to "arouse the voice

---

[31] "Words need silence in which to sound. The most powerful words lead inward to silence. At the heart of them there is a still point. It is there the *Logos* is. When material words have led to the threshold of that sanctuary they should be muted. Ritual always aimed at that *silentium mysticum*.... At the right moment silence is more sublime than words. And this kind of silence is not created to order by self-conscious moments when 'a period of silence is observed'." (Thomas Finan, *Collected Writings*, ed. D. Vincent Twomey, S.V.D. [Dublin, 2019], 438.)

[32] Ratzinger, *Feast of Faith*, 123.

[33] Ibid., 124.

[34] Ibid.

of the cosmos and, by glorifying the Creator, elicit
the glory of the cosmos itself, making it also glorious, beautiful, habitable and beloved."[35] How can
the Church fulfill her mission to humanize the world
if she turns her back on beauty, "which is so closely
allied to love"?[36]

5. The council called for due respect to be shown to
the musical traditions of other religions in mission
lands and urges their incorporation into Church life
after a due process of purification. What is strange,
Ratzinger observes, is that many seem to have forgotten that the countries of Europe also have a
musical inheritance that plays "a great part in their
religious and social life" (SC 119), one that sprang
from the very heart of the Church and her faith.

[35] Ibid.
[36] Ibid.

Chapter Five

SACRED RITUAL

*The demise of rituals in a group not merely forecasts but is
the beginning of social dissolution—because rituals are wholly
necessary for sustaining relations among members of a group and
between groups on the deepest level of value coherence. Rituals are
both signs and causes of such relations, but they are not substitutes
for them.*

—Aidan Kavanagh

*Cult is the root of contemplation; but cult needs contemplation, if
it is not to congeal into ritualism.*

—Joseph Ratzinger

With the reform of the liturgy, to put it mildly, rubrics
seem to have fallen somewhat into disrepute. Before the
council, great attention was given to every detail of these
rituals, particularly those prescribed for the celebration of
Holy Mass. This often led to scrupulosity and a concern
for regulating the details that, some might say, matched
that of the scribes and Pharisees in the New Testament.
That is understandable, considering the legalistic mindset
of the day in the moral theology of the manuals, with its
focus primarily on sin, and considering the fact that liturgy
was regulated primarily by Canon Law. It is of note that
a special section of the general instruction of the so-called

Tridentine Missal was devoted to alerting celebrants in particular to the possible defects that could be made during the celebration of the Mass (and so possible sins that could be committed).[1] Cardinal Godfried Danneels once commented how in the past rubrics dominated everything. "For want of being enlightened, priests formerly executed their actions with 'puerile' obedience." Today, however, the cardinal fears that quite the opposite applies: "It is the liturgy which must obey us and be adapted to our concerns, to the extent of becoming more like a political meeting or a 'happening'."[2] Whatever reservations we may have of his use of the word "puerile", Danneels put his finger on the central problem with the way the liturgical reform was carried out. Those who put into practice the initial reform of the liturgy often paid but minimum attention to the new and simplified rubrics. In the place of obedience to the prescribed actions, some priests valued creativity,[3] paying special attention to increased external activity, together with adaptation to local culture and circumstances. The general rubric, if one may use the term in its loose form, used to justify this new emphasis was *participatio actuosa*, generally translated as active participation,[4]

---

[1] Cf. the eighth edition of the Missal of Pius X, *De Defectibus in Celebratione Missarum Occurentibus*, 61*–64*.

[2] Ryan Topping, "How Liturgy Transforms: Cult and the Renewal of Catholic Culture: The Mass of the Ages", *Fellowship of Catholic Scholars Quarterly* 34/2 (2011): 29, quotations taken from Jonathan Robinson, *The Mass and Modernity: Walking to Heaven Backward* (San Francisco: Ignatius Press, 2005), 31.

[3] According to Ratzinger, creativity is a word that developed within the Marxist world view. "Creativity means that in a universe that in itself is meaningless and came into existence through blind evolution, man can creatively fashion a new and better world" (Ratzinger, *The Spirit of the Liturgy*, trans. John Saward [San Francisco: Ignatius Press, 2000], 168).

[4] For an excellent outline of Ratzinger's critical understanding of *participatio actuosa*, see Mariusz Biliniewicz, *The Liturgical Vision of Pope Benedict XVI: A Theological Inquiry* (Oxford: Peter Lang, 2013), 56–59.

as highlighted by the council's Constitution on the Sacred Liturgy.[5] "Mother Church earnestly desires that all the faithful should be led to that fully conscious, and active participation in the liturgical celebrations which is demanded by the very nature of the liturgy. Such participation by the Christian people as 'a chosen race, a royal priesthood, a holy nation, a redeemed people' (1 Pet. 2:9; cf. 2:4–5), is their right and duty by reason of their baptism."[6]

What did the council mean?

According to Alcuin Reid,[7] the general aim of the Liturgical Movement, stretching from the eighteenth century to the eve of the council, was to restore "liturgical piety in the faithful". To this end, "priests promoted active participation in the liturgy by *distributing liturgical books* among the laity [i.e., the educated laity]". Further, "The Church's pastors hoped that a *more intelligent participation* in the liturgy would help counteract the secularizing influence of the modern age."[8] Commenting on this, Topping

---

[5] Chapter 1 of *Sacrosanctum concilium* is entitled "General Principles for the Restoration and Promotion of the Sacred Liturgy". It is divided into three parts, the second of which is given the title: "The Promotion of Liturgical Instruction and Active Participation" (*SC* 14–20).

[6] *SC* 14.

[7] Alcuin Reid, *The Organic Development of the Liturgy*, 62–67, as quoted by Topping, "How Liturgy Transforms". The following is indebted to Topping. See Alcuin Reid, "*Ut mens nostra concordet voci nostrae*: Sacred Music and Actual Participation in the Liturgy", in Janet E. Rutherford, ed., *Benedict XVI and Beauty in Sacred Music: Proceedings of the Third Fota International Liturgical Conference* (Dublin and New York: Four Courts Press and Sceptre Publishers, 2012), 93–126, esp. 94–95; 104–5.

[8] Topping, "How Liturgy Transforms", 28 (my emphasis). A conference on the history of the liturgy held in the Roman Institute of the Görres Gesellschaft November 20–24, 2021, examined the extent to which the [populist] Zeitgeist influenced the German liturgical movement in both Catholic and Lutheran traditions; this was seen, for example, in the uncritical emphasis on the *Volkskirche* ("people's Church" as over against the "clerical Church"), the *Volksaltar* (altar facing the people), etc. See the interview with one of the organizers,

notes that "Ironically the call for the 'active participation of the faithful' has been deployed for opposite purposes", since it "quickly became identified with external movement rather than an interior action, prayer."[9]

It is interesting to note that, apart from its aim to restore liturgical "piety", the other aim of the preconciliar Liturgical Movement was to achieve a more "intelligent" participation, presumably by clerics and the (more educated?) faithful. Does this betray the cultural influence of the Enlightenment and its aftermath, rationalism? Cardinal Danneels, we saw, described preconciliar priests who followed the rubrics with puerile obedience as being "unenlightened". In the first flush of reform, the primary aim seems to have been to make the ritual of the Mass as *intelligible* as possible. In addition to the banality of the first English translation, didacticism dominated the liturgy, not least in terms of preaching a political message; homilies became more and more moralizing; sacred music became mere performance (with applause for the most entertaining performances), while new "symbols" had to be created to convey new meanings, very often of the most trivial nature (like releasing balloons to mark Easter).

Behind this development was the assumption that participation should be primarily rational. Of the three adjectives used to qualify active participation in the conciliar text, the one that was stressed, at least initially, was "conscious", understood primarily, it would seem, in terms of the greater intelligibility of the ritual text. With the

---

Dr. Stephan Heid, in *Die Tagespost*, December 2, 2021. It is not surprising, then, that the Abbey of Maria Laach, one of the centers of the Catholic Liturgical Movement, initially supported Hitler's Third Reich; cf. Marcel Albert, *Die Benediktinerabtei Maria Laach und der Nationalsozialismus* (Paderborn: Ferdinand Schöningh, 2004).

[9] Ibid.

introduction of the vernacular as the ritual language, liturgists wanted to make the text as intelligible as possible to as
many of the faithful as possible, whatever their educational
background. When that failed, as fail it must, the stress
went on endless commentaries (by the main celebrant) on
the readings or on external actions such as more and more
activities involving the laity: elaborate Offertory proces-
sions, dramatic presentations of the Gospel story, etc., usually succumbing to the temptation to make the Mass as
entertaining as possible or to bring home a moral message.
The object of all these activities was to get the faithful as
fully "involved" as possible, in particular, to get the children "involved".

Did they work? Topping answers by posing a rhetor-
ical question: "Why do so many Catholics stay in bed
on Sunday?" And he gives one possible answer: "Having permitted indifference to rubrics, having perpetuated
a new clericalism, having promoted a misguided activism,
we have deployed liturgy for alien purposes and now too
often reap what we have sown." The question then is:
What is the fundamental purpose of liturgy?

❧ ❧ ❧

Is there an alternative to the prevailing rationalist/utilitar-
ian understanding of *participatio actuosa*? I think there is. It
is related to the true nature of celebration and the nature of
ritual, both of which find their expression in the humble
though complex rubrics that have been honed by tradition.
It was fidelity to these rubrics that enabled the theology
of the sacraments, above all the Mass, to be experienced
by the faithful over the centuries as *sursum corda*, something
that lifts us out of the realm of the mundane and enables
us to encounter the Holy. That experience of encounter

with the Holy, I dare to suggest, is what is truly meant by full, conscious, active participation.

A Philosophy of Celebration

As Aristotle perceived it, contemplation is the highest form of activity.[10] One might say that contemplation is the fullest form of consciousness. For Aristotle, contemplation is the end product of a life of virtue. In ritual, contemplation is adoration, the end product of faith and virtue. The essential point to be stressed at this stage is that genuine ritual lifts people out of the realm of everyday, humdrum reality into the sacral realm. This has been the experience of man since the beginning of time, but it is in the Church that it reached its fullest expression.

Josef Pieper translates Aristotle's term for "contemplation" with "leisure", a term that embraces all truly human activities that are hugely significant but are without purpose—literally devoid of utility—as they serve no purpose beyond their own enjoyment, as in the arts, in sport, and in true celebration. "The true existential poverty of [contemporary] man consists in his having lost the power to celebrate a festival festively."[11] By "feast" here, Pieper means those communal celebrations (at the core of which is some form of cult) that enable us to touch the sacred (Truth, Goodness, Beauty) and so rise above the mundane with the concomitant experience that life is worth living. Modern man is incapable of authentic celebration, Pieper claims, because of two interrelated cultural

---

[10] *Nicomachean Ethics*, bk. 10, vii (1177 a).
[11] Josef Pieper, *In Tune with the World: A Theory of Festivity*, trans. Richard and Clara Winston (Chicago: Franciscan Herald Press, 1973), 44.

forces: an overemphasis placed on work (activity) and an unfathomable experience of life as ultimately absurd (as expressed by J. P. Sartre). As a result, our vision of what it means to be human is to see ourselves, not as *homo sapiens*, but as *homo faber*, the maker of things. As a consequence, all human activity (even the arts) is understood exclusively in functional terms: it must serve some purpose, the most prevalent being economic advantage. Pope Saint Paul VI, in his homily at the end of the council (December 7, 1965), reminded the Council Fathers that the council had occurred at a time when man's focus on the kingdom of earth—man's forgetfulness of God—had become habitual. Because of the age we live in, the question of God became the central point of the council. He added: "[T]he effort to look on him, and to center our heart in him, which we call contemplation, is the highest, the most perfect act of the human spirit, the act which even today can and must be at the apex of all human activity from which human beings receive their dignity."[12]

Due to the influence of such cultural assumptions expressed in the notion of *homo faber* or *homo technicus*, liturgy was, and continues to be, seen as just another form of manmade activity. The various liturgical ministries are understood in functional terms exclusively, so that neither the liturgy in general nor the priesthood in particular can any longer be understood by modern man in sacramental terms. Perhaps this is the real reason for the general misunderstanding of what the council meant by "full, conscious and active participation" in the liturgy. To recover its true meaning, we have to probe behind the superficial

---

[12] *AAS* 58 (1966): 52–53, as quoted by Pope Benedict XVI on October 10, 2012, in his address on the eve of the fiftieth anniversary of Vatican II that marked the opening of the Year of Faith.

understanding of liturgy in terms of intelligibility and discover once again what it means to say that liturgy is the ritual celebration of the sacraments.

An Anthropology of Ritual

To understand the intrinsic relationship between liturgy and the sacraments, it is necessary to rediscover the central role played by ritual in human life and society. By ritual is meant, strictly speaking, those communal rites that make leisure possible in the profound sense once described by Josef Pieper as follows (taking his cue from Nietzsche): leisure is the effect of those experiences that enable us to affirm that life is worth living. This should be the experience evoked by all the sacraments in various degrees, but above all by the Rite of the Mass, at the core of which is the efficacious memorial of the sacrifice of Jesus Christ. For it is the salvific sacrifice of Jesus that enables us to affirm unconditionally that life is truly good, is truly worth living in such a way that we can face whatever the future might bring with that hope which cannot disappoint us "because God's love has been poured into our hearts through the Holy Spirit who has been given to us" (Rom 5:5).

According to Joseph Ratzinger,[13] we find in the most archaic cultures something like a basic pattern of the Christian sacraments. As we have indicated already, these are the ritual responses of mankind to those nodal points (*Knotenpunkte*) of human experience which, according to Schleiermacher, open man up to the mystery of his existence and make him transparent for Transcendence.

---

[13] "The Sacramental Foundation of Christian Existence", in *JRCW* 11:153–68.

These nodal points are not intellectual by nature but arise, in the first instance, directly from man's biological existence (birth, death, puberty, marriage, meals); secondly, from the experience of man's historicity (guilt); and finally from those events that determine the continuation in existence of the body politic (the inauguration of kings and priests). Ratzinger here is consciously trying to counter the dualistic assumptions of post-Enlightenment culture that spirit can only be encountered by spirit.[14] These primal human experiences arising from our bodily, historical, and social nature at certain pivotal moments in life demand to be celebrated with corresponding rites and rituals. In this regard, one could quote Saint Paul: "But it is not the spiritual which is first but the physical, and then the spiritual" (1 Cor 15:46). As the ethnologists have discovered, these primal rites and rituals are communal by nature, vouchsafed for by sacred tradition, and spiritually effective thanks to a divine origin in the form of a creation myth. The communal rituals are responses to primordial experiences that touch, not some aspect of our lives, but our basic humanity in its totality. The rituals open us up to what transcends our mundane existence and, in so doing, create a bond among the participants in the rites that makes life worth living at a personal and communal level. These rites are constituted by symbols—gestures and languages that are dense in meaning—which point beyond themselves to what gives meaning to human existence.

Mircea Eliade discovered in his study of world religions that behind the rites of initiation in all cultures is the assumption that one becomes human only by encounter with the divine. Anthropologists have discovered that a

---

[14] "The error of anti-sacramental idealism consists in the fact that it wants to make man into a pure spirit in God's sight" (ibid., 166).

community renews itself periodically by participation in initiation rites and other related rites, such as arise from the experience of human guilt or the inauguration of a new king. The structure of these rites is such that they produce that experience of liminality which opens us up to the supra-mundane. These rites also betray a symbolism that is universally valid, reflecting in various ways that primordial experience of death and rebirth through that awe-filled encounter with the Holy described by Rudolf Otto,[15] which experience constitutes us as human beings. It is not surprising that Saint Ephraim the Syrian could affirm that the symbols of Christ are imprinted in creation (*De virginitate*, 6:7), since, as we read in the Prologue to Saint John, the whole of creation bears the impress of the Divine *Logos* (Jn 1:3) and so is orientated to him. Ratzinger affirms that ritual symbols belong to the treasury of the nations, which reflect the wisdom of God. As a result, by means of the unitary language of symbols, the Christian finds access to the sacraments of creation present in the natural religions.[16] Ratzinger calls it the anti-Marcion aspect of the Catholic theory of cult.

However, Ratzinger also stresses how the symbolic language of the rites of the natural religions were radically transformed by God's self-revelation in the process of history. Christianity is distinguished from the natural religions in two ways. First of all, it approaches them in a way that purifies and sanctifies them, and indeed this was already

---

[15] Rudolf Otto, *The Idea of the Holy: An Inquiry into the Non-rational Factor in the Idea of the Divine and Its Relation to the Rational*, trans. John W. Harvey, 2nd ed. (London: Oxford University Press, 1950).

[16] "The symbols of creation are signs pointing to Christ, and Christ is the fulfillment not only of history but also of creation: In him who is the *mysterium* of God, everything attains its unity" (Ratzinger, "On the Concept of Sacrament", *JRCW* 11:184, emphasis in text).

the case in the Old Testament. "All Jewish festivals ... have a triple basis. The initial stratum is composed of feasts of nature religion, which connect with creation and with man's search for God through creation; this then develops into feasts of remembrance, of the recollection and making-present of God's saving deeds; finally, remembering increasingly takes on the form of hope for the coming definitive saving deed that is still awaited."[17]

Secondly, Christianity does not appeal to the cosmos (or immanent cosmic forces of which we are part and which find expression in myth) but to a historical event. Myths exclude factual history, while Christianity appeals to what has actually happened, since God took the initiative and intervened in history. Christianity is *memoria* of history.[18] And so, history becomes salvific, and the events that constitute salvation history are seen to be part of God's design, giving rise to an interpretation of salvation history that is typological. By typological is meant the unique scriptural way of understanding words and events of the Old Testament as anticipating or pointing to—and only fully understood in the light of—their fulfillment in the words and life of Jesus Christ and his Body, the Church. Ratzinger concludes that the typological reading of Scripture is the interior source of the Church's notion of sacrament. Going to church to worship, Ratzinger wrote, means "inserting myself into God's history with man by which I as a human being attain my true human existence and which, for that reason, alone

---

[17] Benedict XVI, *Jesus of Nazareth: From the Baptism in the Jordan to the Transfiguration* (New York: Doubleday, 2007), 237–38; see also 307.

[18] As Tolkien quipped to C. S. Lewis, myth could be a "memoria of history" and its deep significance. I am grateful to John Hogan for reminding me of this: https://www.catholiceducation.org/en/culture/art/j-r-r-tolkien-truth-and-myth.html.

opens up to me the true space for my encounter with God's eternal love."[19] That insertion is by way of the concrete liturgical acts of Christian initiation—baptism, confirmation, and Eucharist.

In the rites of Christian initiation, cosmic symbols, such as water (primarily understood as a symbol of death and rebirth), become the means of insertion into God's design for mankind realized in Jesus Christ and effectively present in the universal community that is the Church. Already in the New Testament, we have the correspondence of the events of salvation history and the sacrament of initiation, as, for example, between:

> the Flood (1 Pet 3:20–21),
> > → the Red Sea (1 Cor 10:1f.),
> > > → the Baptism of Jesus and his suffering
> > > (Mk 10:38, Lk 12:50; Jn 19:34),
> > > > → and our baptism (Rom 6:4).

All that needs to be stressed at this point is the fact that the Christian sacraments are specific rites that in various ways have their origin in their ritual language of our common humanity. Since man is of his very nature religious, he has his own "language" that can express this dimension of his being. That is what we mean by ritual. This "language" remains valid for all time, even when purified and transformed by being taken up and inserted into God's history with man that has its center in Christ. The same truth is attested in the mention in the Roman Canon of the sacrifice of Abel and that of Abraham as well as the sacrifice of the pagan high priest Melchizedek, all of which mark the transition from natural religious cults to the rites of salvation history.

---

[19] "Sacramental Foundation of Christian Existence", *JRCW* 11:168 (revised translation).

Rubrics and *Participatio Actuosa*

Victor Turner, who with his wife, Edith, was the founder of the post-structuralist study of ritual, to whom I am indebted for much of the above, published an article in 1976 in the liturgical journal *Worship*,[20] expressing his concern about the liturgical reform. A "Catholic by faith and anthropologist by profession", as he said, he "could hardly be unmoved by the many changes introduced into the Roman Rite after the Second Vatican Council." He feared that, because of contemporary secularist tendencies, the dynamics of authentic ritual were being lost. The same ritual dynamics that he had discovered in his study of ritual in so-called primitive religions, Turner recognized, were also characteristic of the Tridentine Rite in its fullness. He attributed this to the rich and complex rubrics that had been formed, refined, and perfected over thousands of years by the Catholic genius, as he called it. The end product of strict adhesion to these rubrics was the experience of what Turner called *communitas*.[21]

[20] Victor Turner, "Ritual, Tribal and Catholic", *Worship* 50 (1970): 504–26. For an account of the life and work of Victor Turner and his wife, Edith, see Sohrab Ahmari, *The Unbroken Thread: Discovering the Wisdom of Tradition in an Age of Chaos* (London: Hodder & Stoughton, 2021), 85–102; see also the paper on Turner's writings read by Mary Collins to the North American Academy of Liturgy (January 5–8, 1976) entitled: "Ritual Symbols and the Ritual Process: The Work of Victor W. Turner", *Worship* 50/4 (1976): 336–46, together with John H. McKenna's summary of the discussion on the question of ritual gesture and activity that her paper provoked (ibid., 347–52).

[21] See Victor W. Turner, *The Ritual Process: Structure and Anti-Structure* (New York: Aldine Publishing, 1969), especially 131–65. Of particular interest is the *Chihamba* ritual of the Ndembu tribe of central southern Africa, in which the Turners were invited to participate. It triggered their conversion from atheism to faith. In Ahmari's words: "The ritual the Turners had witnessed was elaborate, obscure, now sad, now humorous, now terrifying—and strangely familiar: A god submits willingly to humiliation and death, thus redeeming his mortal fellows. The vessel that was rejected becomes the foundation of a new, fertile *communitas*. Where had the Turners heard all this before?" (Ahmari, *Unbroken Thread*, 96).

Communitas is a sense of oneness among the participants in the ritual, thanks to their taking part in a predetermined rite that is familiar to them and yet conveys the liminal experience of transcending the mundane for the duration of the ritual, familiarity being the hallmark of ritual. But the effect of authentic ritual spills over into their daily life, since it gives ultimate meaning to their lives as individuals and in common. The effectiveness of the ritual is due in great part to the regular repetition of the same rite that, apart from insignificant changes, is understood by all participants as unalterable by those responsible for conducting the rituals: all must abide by the (mostly unwritten) rubrics. "For authentic ritual is the reflexive outcome of the passionate thought and experiential wisdom of many together through many generations of shared and directly transmitted social life."[22] I would like to suggest that what Turner calls *communitas*—and what Pieper called "leisure"—could be understood as the effect of *participatio actuosa*, properly understood as the apt performance of ritual. It is of note that, according to Ratzinger, it was the paschal sacrifice at Sinai (the goal of the Exodus) that effected the formation of the Chosen People as a people. "In this is expressed a primordial knowledge of humanity, one encountered ever again in the history of religion, [namely,] that freedom and the formation of community are ultimately to be obtained, not through the use of force or through mere industry, but through a love that becomes sacrificial and that first binds men together in their depths because it lets them touch the dimension of the divine."[23]

[22] Turner, "Ritual, Tribal and Catholic", 507.
[23] Ratzinger, "Freedom and Liberation", in his *Church, Ecumenism, and Politics: New Endeavors in Ecclesiology*, trans. Michael J. Miller et al. (San Francisco: Ignatius Press, 2008), 250.

Commenting on the rituals of the Ndembu, Turner writes: "I found in them affinities with the pre-conciliar rites of the Catholic Church—as well as striking differences. These ritual systems had more in common than either has with the post-conciliar Catholic liturgy."[24] After describing these similarities and differences in some detail, he comments: "Perhaps the major distinction between the tribal and the universalistic ritual systems is that the former are transmitted by oral tradition and the latter by written, later printed rubrics."[25] However, what he terms the "Archimedean point" of tribal ritual (and by extension, *mutatis mutandis*, all ritual) is "the collective performance itself, not the general performative rules". The success of a performance consists in "how it tallies, to the satisfaction of the participants, present experiences with traditional wisdom". Tribal rules, he also observed, contain constant and variable features. The constant features include dominant symbols and clustering of symbolic actions, while the variable features include passages of spontaneous symbolic action.

How was it that Turner found significant compatibility between Ndembu and preconciliar ritual as ritual processes (though not, understandably, in creedal terms)? "In the first place, the Catholic Church used to possess [sic] great skill in mediating between universal and particular modes of religious experience. Even although writing introduces rubrical rigidity in place of oral flexibility, the Church compensated for this by the sheer versatility of its internal differentiation."[26]

Turner stresses that ritual must be understood as a process or performance with its own inherent dynamics:

[24] Ibid., 506.
[25] Ibid., 508.
[26] Ibid., 509.

Just as language has a set of rules and a lexicon of words which may be arrayed in various ways to generate "messages", intelligible sentences, so, it might be said, the language of ritual depends upon "syntactical" rules and possesses a "lexicon" of both verbal and non-verbal terms, which may be varyingly arrayed to communicate messages, in the form of ritual processes, about the supreme message of Christ to the world.

Turner continues:

Theorists of the new discipline of "communications" might regard ritual as an extreme case of "redundancy", saying the same thing in numerous ways. But this is precisely where ritual ceases to be merely "*cognitive*," and becomes "*supersaturated*" with "*existence*". The whole person is impregnated with a single message through all the channels of communication available to him. He has to *live* what is being communicated not merely *understand* it.[27]

In Turner's description of a successful ritual, the central term he uses is "flow". This is a technical term developed by Professor Mihaly Csikszentmihalyi of the University of Chicago. For him, "flow" is:

a state in which action follows action according to an internal logic which seems to need no conscious intervention on our part; we experience it as a unified flowing from one moment to the next, in which we feel in control of our actions, and in which there is little difference between self and environment, between stimulus and response, or between past, present and future. He sees flow as a common experience whenever people act

---

[27] Ibid., 510 [emphasis mine].

with total involvement, whether in play or sport, in the creative experience in art and literature, or in religious experience.[28]

"Total involvement" of this nature would seem to be what the council proposed as full, conscious and active participation in the liturgy.

What is fascinating is how, after giving an overview of the rich complexity of rubrics that governed the preconciliar liturgy, Turner still managed to see an affinity between it and the looser rituals of an African tribe based on oral tradition. He explains this by drawing on his own experience on returning to England from his fieldwork in Africa, when he attended a Mass on the Feast of All Saints in a working-class parish in Stockport, Cheshire. The priest was a newly ordained Irish priest, no great doctor of the Church and no nightingale, but, nonetheless, Turner "felt in the texture of his performance something of the same deep contact with the human condition tinged with transcendence that I had experienced in central Africa when I attended rituals presided over by dedicated ritual specialists."[29] He noted not only the sincerity of the priest but the bond between priest and congregation that had been molded by innumerable participations in "a throng of believers who seemed at times to epitomize the true Church: militant, suffering and triumphant". Such a community could only have been formed by the availability to priest and people of "a collective vehicle, the inspired artwork of ages, which gave magisterial form to their pure, immediate insights". He concluded that: "It was this quality of union between past inspiration, bodied

[28] Ibid., 520.
[29] Ibid., 516.

in ritual forms and symbols, and present experience, person by person, of bereavements and other sufferings, the whole added up to a divine-human meaning beyond any individual's experience, which I detected in the ritual lives both of African peasants and Lancastrian proletarians."[30]

One sentence of that quote deserves to be underlined. Turner says that he "felt in the texture of his performance something of the same deep contact with the human condition tinged with transcendence that I had experienced in central Africa when I attended rituals presided over by dedicated ritual specialists." It was this something that Pieper called leisure—a liminal experience where all mundane differences—such as class and education—were transcended in the solemn, authentic ritual celebration on a Feast Day.

Turner's critique has many implications. As early as 1971, Aidan Kavanagh pleaded with his fellow liturgists to pay attention to, among other things (such as cosmology and ecclesiology), the findings of anthropologists of ritual.[31] One positive result of these findings was to help liturgists rediscover the perennial significance of the arcane discipline in the early Church for initiating converts, which in turn helped shape the present Rite of Christian Initiation for Adults. Another even more important implication is the insight that ritual is rooted in particular communities united by personal and communal experiences—or, rather, it would be more accurate to say that ritual, responding to the deepest human needs and experiences, shapes particular communities and so, in the last analysis, cannot be really understood or, more importantly, truly appreciated

---

[30] Ibid., 516–17.

[31] Cf. Aidan Kavanagh, "Relevance and Change in the Liturgy", *Worship* 45/2 (1971). This short article should be required reading for all who exercise various liturgical ministries but above all for the priest-celebrant.

in abstraction from those communities. For this reason, we can see the wisdom of Pope Benedict XVI's Motu Proprio *Summorum Pontificum*, which, while removing the restrictions on the use of the Extraordinary Form of the Roman Rite, required that special parish churches be delegated for its regular use. This was needed so that communities could be formed in and by the Extraordinary Form.

With regard to the Ordinary Form of the Roman Rite, we must ask whether "the texture of its performance" conveys "something of the same deep contact with the human condition tinged with transcendence" that Turner experienced both in the tribal rites and in the preconciliar Mass in Stockport. I think that it can and, in fact does (at least on occasion), for the majority of believers who have remained faithful despite suffering from neo-clerical creativity. On the other hand, it must be admitted, as Topping claims, that "[m]any of us have forgotten why Catholics worship at all. We have forgotten not only the sacrificial nature of the Mass but also how the Mass relates to the soup kitchen."[32] He sees the casual approach of priests to the liturgy as the main obstacle to authentic Catholic worship:

> If you no longer see yourself as the servant of a tradition but its master, no longer believe that the rubrics veil a mystery, that the soul requires truth to be wrapped in the garment of beauty, then quite reasonably you are likely to treat the Mass more as a gathering of friends than as a sacrifice of God. Others catch on. Most move on. And, insofar as liturgy is mined for alien purposes, its capacity to excite as the source and summit of our salvation diminishes.[33]

[32] Topping, "How Liturgy Transforms", 30. See the *cri de coeur* of one such "ordinary Catholic", as she calls herself: Mary E. Kearns, *Has Some Enemy Done This?* (Athy: Lumen Fidei Press, 2016).

[33] Topping, "How Liturgy Transforms", 30.

Rubrics and the Ordinary Form
of the Roman Rite

When the celebrant and other participants treat the rubrics with due respect, they acknowledge in effect that the divine liturgy is precisely that: a form of worship that is of divine institution and efficacy and, so, not at our disposal. Admittedly, the Ordinary Form of the Roman Rite allows for "certain accommodations and adaptations" that are "specified in this General Instruction and in the Order of Mass".[34] However, as *The General Instruction of the Roman Missal*, more or less quoting *Sacrosanctum Concilium* 22, points out unequivocally: "The priest must remember that he is the servant of the sacred Liturgy and that he himself is not permitted, on his own initiative, to add, to remove, or to change anything in the celebration of Mass."[35] Obedience to the rubrics calls, not for enlightenment, but for humble submission to what is not at our disposal.[36] They help the priest in particular to be attentive to what he is about, as, for example, the rubric that, after the Consecration, he raises the consecrated Host and chalice and silently displays it to the congregation, he genuflects and *adores*. Other examples are the prayers the celebrant says silently at the *Lavabo* (reminding *himself* of his sinfulness) or after the *Agnus Dei* (to prepare *himself* interiorly before proclaiming to the faithful: "Behold the Lamb of God"), and the prayer

---

[34] *The General Instruction of the Roman Missal*, no. 23.

[35] Ibid., no. 24.

[36] "The life of the liturgy does not come from what dawns upon the minds of individuals and planning groups. On the contrary, it is God's descent upon our world, the source of real liberation. He alone can open the door to freedom. The more priests and faithful humbly surrender themselves to this descent of God, the more 'new' the liturgy will constantly be, and the more true and personal it becomes" (Ratzinger, *Spirit of the Liturgy*, 168–69).

to be said by the priest "quietly" (in thanksgiving) after purifying the chalice, paten, and ciborium—incidentally, one of the most beautiful texts in the English translation, but rarely used.[37]

That said, one must also ask whether or not some rubrics need to be revised; such, of course, can only be undertaken by apostolic authority (the pope or an episcopal conference) and *not* by the celebrant himself. One major change that is in need of reconsideration is the practice of the celebrant facing the people for the entire duration of the Mass. Though not advocated by the council, this posture became widespread after the initial reform was put into practice. The theological reasons for the ancient rubric of celebrating *ad orientem* are familiar, and so we can leave them aside.[38] Some liturgists try to justify facing the people primarily in terms of an understanding of the Eucharist as meal. Indeed, that is one possible interpretation of the *General Instruction*, which states that the altar, "on which is effected the Sacrifice of the Cross made present under sacramental signs, is also the table of the Lord to which the People of God is convoked to participate in the Mass".[39] The same instruction also rules that "the altar should be built ... in such a way that ... Mass can be celebrated facing the people, which

[37] "What has passed our lips as food, O Lord,
　　may we possess in purity of heart,
　　that what has been given to us in time
　　may be our healing for eternity."

[38] See above, chap. 1, note 6. It should be noted that the Catholic Church is the only Christian faith-community that celebrates *versus populum*, a fact that also has serious implications for ecumenism (cf. Kurt Cardinal Koch, "Gabe und Aufgabe: Roms Liturgiereformen in ökumenischer Perspektive", in Stephan Heid, ed., *Operation am lebenden Objekt: Roms Liturgiereformen von Trient bis zum Vaticanum II* [Berlin, 2014], 16).

[39] *The General Instruction of the Roman Missal*, no. 296.

is desirable wherever possible."⁴⁰ This recommendation, not of the council but of those appointed to implement its decisions, soon became *de rigueur*. However, it would seem that those liturgical experts based their interpretation on the false assumption that facing the people was the original way Mass was celebrated, an assumption that has since been proved to be totally without any historical foundation whatsoever.⁴¹ One anthropologist suggested that the reason why such radical departures from tradition caught on so quickly was because they fit into the culture of modern technological society, which is essentially that of people without roots and, so, nomadic in nature.⁴² Nomads do not build sacral buildings. Their rituals are celebrated around a fire, where the members of the tribe gather for mutual support.

Be that as it may, the most important effect of the priest facing the congregation for the entire Mass is the way it affects the priest himself, namely, the *ars celebrandi*. Instead of leading the congregation into a dialogue with God (worship and adoration), there is a temptation to enter into dialogue with those now facing him. Facing the congregation, it seems to me, albeit with some qualification, may be suitable for the first part, the Liturgy of the Word. But facing the congregation for the whole celebration of the Eucharist makes it difficult to avoid the personality

⁴⁰ Ibid., no. 299.
⁴¹ Stephan Heid, *Altar und Kirche: Prinzipien christlicher Liturgie*, 2nd ed. (Regensburg: Schnell & Steiner, 2019), concluded his detailed analysis of the historical and theological evidence with the blunt assertion that: "The contemporary people's altar (*Volksaltar*), be it round or rectangular, is the product of historical misinformation or else historical archaism. To claim such an altar as the centre of the eucharistic table fellowship in the early Church is a scholarly fiction" (p. 464).
⁴² See Mary Douglas, *Natural Symbols: Explorations in Cosmology* (Barrie and Rockliff: Cresset Press, 1970).

of the celebrant becoming central to the celebration—
especially if the celebrant has an outgoing personality or is
prone to narcissism. This in turn feeds into the tendency
to turn the Mass into an occasion to teach or, worse, into
a form of entertainment (with the main celebrant becoming in effect the master of ceremonies). In either case, the
sacrificial nature of the Mass is downplayed.

In the history of religious rituals all over the world,
those individuals (priests, druids, shamans) who represent
the world of the sacred are always masked. This is because the celebrant's own personality vanishes behind the
deity he represents. The Greek term for the masks used
in religious rites (and so in the theatre that emerged from
the rites) is *persona*. So, apart from theological reasons,
there is, therefore, also a ritual or anthropological reason
for the Church's teaching that certain vestments are prescribed for the priest who acts *in persona Christi*. Vestments
(all of which are dense in meanings, now largely forgotten
but retrievable) are the equivalent of the mask in tribal
and other rites. Accordingly, in the Extraordinary Form
of the Roman Rite, the face of the celebrant is rarely
seen; what is mostly seen is the elaborately decorated back
of his chasuble. Facing the east symbolically represents
our turning toward the Risen Christ coming in glory and
present in the sacrifice of the Mass. Facing east together
with the congregation, the priest, like Moses, leads his
people into the Promised Land, leads the congregation to
encounter the awaited Risen Lord, who becomes present
on the altar at the Consecration. What is important here
is that, for the priest himself, this way of celebrating the
Mass from the Offertory on to the Communion, lends
itself to his addressing God in prayer and so promotes his
own authentic worship and adoration—as well as that of
the faithful present.

116

Ritual and Sacrifice

Ratzinger draws attention to the revolutionary nature of Scripture's understanding of expiation and redemption, as compared with that found in non-Christian religions.

Almost all religions center around the problem of expiation; they arise out of man's knowledge of his guilt before God and signify the attempt to remove this feeling of guilt, to surmount the guilt through conciliatory actions offered up to God. The expiatory activity by which men hope to conciliate the Divinity and to put him in a gracious mood stands at the heart of the history of religion.[43]

In the New Testament, the reverse is the case. It is not man who seeks expiation, but God who comes to man with it. "[God] restores disturbed right on the initiative of his own power to love, by making unjust man just again, the dead living again, through his own creative mercy. His righteousness is grace."[44] The New Testament does not say that men appease God, but the very opposite: "[In] Christ God was reconciling the world to himself" (2 Cor 5:19). This is a radical break within the history of religions: God does not wait for the guilty to approach him; He takes the initiative and goes to meet them and reconcile them.[45] The Incarnation is directed to the Cross. Thus, it appears primarily as a movement from above. "It stands there, not as the work of expiation that mankind offers to the wrathful God, but as the expression of that foolish love

---

[43] Ratzinger, *Introduction to Christianity*, trans. J.R. Foster (Communio Books; San Francisco: Ignatius Press, 2004), 282.

[44] Ratzinger, Ibid.

[45] However, it would seem that, in the world religions, anticipations of such a divine initiative can be found, as in the case of the *Chihamba* ritual of the Ndembu (see above, note 21).

of God's that gives itself away to the point of humiliation in order thus to save man; it is *his* approach to us, not the other way about."[46] With this radical break with expiation as understood in the history of religions comes a new form of religion as expressed in Christian worship and Christian existence. Worship is now essentially *Eucharistia*, thanksgiving for the divine deed of salvation. "Christian sacrifice does not consist in a giving of what God would not have without us but in our becoming totally receptive and letting ourselves be completely taken over by him. Letting God act on us—that is Christian sacrifice."[47]

The challenge posed by Pope Benedict XVI's "reform of the reform" is to fine-tune the existing rubrics so that, with the primary emphasis on objectivity and receptivity (not creativity), the Mass is once again truly experienced as a ritualized thanksgiving for the majestic divine deed of salvation, the sacrifice of the Mass, the source of the most profound *communitas*—communion with God and with one another in Christ through the action of the Holy Spirit—and the source of her mission.

Pope Benedict XVI's vision of the liturgy dovetails with that of the great American liturgist Aidan Kavanagh, who concluded the Hale Memorial Lectures he gave at Seabury Western Theological Seminary in 1981 as follows:

> I have suggested that there is an inseparable dialectic between liturgy and theology which is basic, fundamental, and primary for the whole of what I have called Christian *orthodoxia*, a life of "right worship", which quite overflows what goes on in churches during divine service to permeate all aspects of the faithful community's daily business.

---

[46] Ratzinger, *Introduction to Christianity*, 283.
[47] Ibid.

All these aspects I aggregated under the term "rite" as a broad designation of the style taken by corporate Christian life in particular circumstances. I tried to emphasize that, while liturgy does not exhaust rite, it does anchor it in the faithful assembly's regular encounter with the living God in Christ through worship in Spirit and in truth.[48]

[48] Aidan Kavanagh, *On Liturgical Theology* (Collegeville, Minn.: Liturgical Press, 1992), 177. Earlier in his seminal 1971 article "Relevance and Change", he concluded by reminding his readers that "Christian worship and community can survive, and has survived, two millennia of being tinkered with by experts.... But it cannot survive without the grim joy of a thoughtful and humane people whose communion in grace and faith is real on all levels of their lives in the world. The gospel is the *only* ultimate summoner of such a people to worship. What they do there is nothing but to celebrate a world made new" (72, emphasis in text).

EXCURSUS

An Amazonian Rite?

In *Querida Amazonia*, Pope Francis noted that fifty years had passed since the Second Vatican Council had called for an effort to be made "to inculturate the liturgy among indigenous peoples".[1] He comments that "we still have far to go along these lines", adding in a footnote (120): "During the Synod, there was a proposal to develop an 'Amazonian rite'." This laconic reference to an Amazonian rite (please note the use of lowercase "r" in Spanish and English) in footnote 120 has been compared to the "breakthrough" with regard to the admittance of remarried divorcees to Holy Communion, which, it is claimed, is implicit in footnote 351 of *Amoris Laetitia*. In the opinion of the Spanish liberation theologian Father Víctor Codina, S.J.[2] (writing in the Amazonian ecclesial network, REPAM), footnote 120's implicit approval of an Amazonian rite is a "breakthrough" insofar as it appears to be an approval for the creation of an Amazonian Rite, which would then allow for both married clergy and female ministers as proposed by the *Final Document* of the Synod of the Amazon (e.g., *FD* 111).[3] Is this the case?

---

[1] He references *SC* 37–40, 65, 77, 81.

[2] Born in 1931, he studied under Karl Rahner, S.J., and was Professor of Theology first in Barcelona (1965) and then in Bolivia (1982–2018).

[3] Cf. https://redamazonica.org/2020/03/un-nuevo-rito-amazonico/

In contrast with the term "rites" (meaning rituals),[4] the term "Rite" (with uppercase "R" in Spanish as in English) is used by Codina in the sense of a *particular Church* that has her own liturgical and theological tradition with her distinctive discipline and organization, such as those Eastern Catholic Churches subject to the Oriental Code of Canon law, which law, of course, allows for married clergy. When the pope mentions the synod's proposal to create an Amazonian rite in footnote 120, he uses the lowercase "r" (En el Sínodo surgió la propuesta de elaborar un "rito amazónico"). Pope Francis would seem to refer solely to the liturgy, which needs to be accommodated to the Amazonian cultures, and not to the creation of a particular Church along the lines of the Oriental Catholic Churches.

What, then, does the *Final Document* propose? It is, to say the least, somewhat ambivalent. Under the subheading "A Rite for indigenous peoples", the *Final Document* 116 states: "The Second Vatican Council created possibilities for liturgical pluralism 'for legitimate variations and adaptations for different groups, regions, and peoples' (*SC* 38)." This, of course, is true, but the *Final Document* omits the important proviso in the conciliar text: "provided that the substantial unity of the Roman rite is preserved." In other words, the council cannot be appealed to as advocating the creation of a new rite comparable to those found in the Oriental Catholic Churches. It allowed for modifications to the Roman Rite, enriching it, so it could resonate with the deeper aspirations of a people's culture,[5] as in the case

---

[4] As used in *Querida Amazonia* 20 with regard to the rituals of Amazonian peoples; see also *The Amazon: New Paths for the Church and for an Integral Economy: Final Document* (October 26, 2019) [hereafter abbreviated FD] 15, 52, 54.

[5] Cf. *SC* 37: "Anything in these people's way of life which is not indissolubly bound up with superstition and error she studies with sympathy and, if possible, preserves intact. Sometimes in fact she admits such things in the liturgy itself, so long as they harmonize with its true and authentic spirit." This would seem

of the Zairean Rite[6] and others in Africa and Asia. However, the *Final Document* fudges the issue in paragraph 117, which allows someone like Father Codina to claim that what is really being proposed is more than a liturgical adaption of the Roman Rite but the formation of a particular Church organization. *FD* 117 draws attention to the fact that: "There are 23 different Rites in the Catholic Church, a clear sign of a tradition that from the first centuries has tried to inculturate the contents of the faith and its celebration through language that coheres as much as possible with the mystery it seeks to … express. All these traditions have their origin in function of the Church's mission". A quotation from *CCC* 1202 is used to support this claim.

What of this claim? To begin with, the number of Rites (23) is misleading (six would be more accurate) since the majority are but variations on the original Byzantine Rite. Others are variations of the Alexandrian Rite or the East and West Syrian Rites. Indeed, though ultimately of apostolic origin, these Oriental Rites can be traced back either to post-Constantinian Antioch or Alexandria (apart, perhaps, from the Armenian Rite, which may be

---

to be echoed in the *Final Document* where it proposes that: "We should give an authentically catholic response to the request of the Amazonian communities to adapt the liturgy by valuing the original worldview, traditions, symbols and rites that include transcendent, community and ecological dimensions" (*FD* 116).

[6] I recall, how, at the annual meeting of his former doctoral students in the autumn of 1987, Cardinal Ratzinger commented favourably on the Zairean rite, which he had experienced in Kinshasa while attending a meeting with the Doctrinal Commissions of Africa. Likewise, John Cavadini, in his defence of Vatican II, wrote: "I attended a Mass celebrated according to the Rite of Zaire in an isolated region of the Democratic Republic of the Congo. It fully expressed the spirit of the liturgy of the universal Church not in spite of its being celebrated in an unmistakably African voicing, but because of it. In chant and in movement it communicated a dignity commensurate with the 'awfulness of the Sacrifice,' as Servant of God Dorothy Day once put it, while clothing it in an un-self-conscious warmth appropriate to the 'Sacrament of Charity'." (https://churchlifejournal.nd.edu/articles/is-vatican-ii-bad-seed/)

traced back to Saints Addai and Mari).[7] What is striking
is that all these Churches claim saints as the originators of
their specific liturgical traditions (e.g., the Divine Liturgies of Saint James, Saint Basil the Great, and Saint John
Chrysostom), which, in the course of the centuries, were
(as was the case of the Western rites such as the Roman,
Gallican, Mozarabic, or Celtic rites) organically developed and gradually enriched by theological reflection and
native cultural developments.[8] They were not the product
of commissions made up of liturgical and other experts
meeting around a large table, whose written text would
be approved by a new regional "episcopal organization"[9]
to be set up ostensibly to coordinate the various dioceses
of Amazonia.

Leaving aside the larger, and perhaps more significant,
question as to the precise nature of the proposed regional
episcopal organization,[10] it seems to me that entrusting the
creation of an Amazonian [liturgical] rite to a committee

[7] See Ratzinger, *The Spirit of the Liturgy*, trans. John Saward (San Francisco:
Ignatius Press, 2000), 169–70 (= *JRCW*, 11:98–105).

[8] See Pope Pius XII in his encyclical *Mediator Dei* (November 20, 1947),
nos. 49–59.

[9] "We propose the creation of a Bishops' organism that ... would be a per-
manent and representative Bishops' organism that promotes synodality in the
Amazon region, connected with CELAM, with its own structure, in a simple organization and also connected with REPAM. So constituted, it can be
the effective instrument in the territory of the Latin American and Caribbean
Church for taking up many of the proposals that emerged in this Synod. It
would be the nexus for developing Church and socio-environmental networks
and initiatives at the continental and international levels" (*FD* 115). Presumably
the unusual term *un organismo episcopal* in the Spanish version should be rendered "an episcopal organization". If so, then this proposal could be interpreted
as advocating an autonomous Amazonian Rite Church.

[10] Does it really mean a particular Church such as the Eastern Catholic
Churches? However, it is obvious that no Eastern Rite Church was ever created by a commission from *tabula rasa* such as proposed by *FD* 115. This again
betrays the modern Western mentality characterized by functionalism.

of experts is the fundamental flaw of the *Final Document*'s recommendation about an Amazonian rite or liturgical practice.[11]

In a sense, the *Final Document*'s proposal about how to develop an autochthonous liturgical rite by means of a *committee* is but a logical conclusion of the main weakness of the *Constitution on the Sacred Liturgy*, which, in turn, shaped its implementation after the council, namely, the modern Western, rationalistic, indeed, functionalistic, approach to liturgy.[12] As pointed out above, if liturgists had known of the nature (i.e., the inner dynamics) of *ritual* as discovered by recently anthropologists, then they would not have made the mistakes in the reform of the liturgy after the council.

---

[11] "The new organism of the Church in the Amazon should establish a competent commission to study and discuss, according to the habits and customs of the ancestral peoples, the elaboration of an Amazonian rite that expresses the liturgical, theological, disciplinary and spiritual patrimony of the Amazon, with special reference to what *Lumen Gentium* affirms for the Oriental Churches (cf. *LG* 23)" (*FD* 119). This paragraph is ambiguous. It could be interpreted to mean that the *FD* was advocating not just an indigenous Amazonian liturgy but a distinct organization ("the new organism") in the sense of a quasi-autonomous Church, an Amazonian Rite like the Eastern Catholic Churches.

[12] See, for example, *FD* 118, which proposes "that the process of inculturation of the faith ... be expressed with the utmost coherence, in order that it may also be celebrated and lived in the languages proper to the Amazon's peoples." The stress on "coherence" and "languages" betrays the post-Enlightenment concern for the intellectual apprehension of the ritual's content—understanding *participatio actuosa* in a rationalist sense—and not the ritual *per se* being comprised of symbolic movements and ritualized gestures as well as a distinct language that expresses the numinous. *FD* 118 adds: "It is urgent to form committees for the translation of biblical and the preparation of liturgical texts in the different local languages." Again, this is a typical modern, Western, rationalistic approach to liturgy. As Ratzinger once commented: "... it seems to me very dangerous to suggest that missionary liturgies could be created overnight, so to speak, by Bishops' Conferences, which would themselves be dependent on memoranda drawn up by academics" (Ratzinger, *The Feast of Faith*, trans. Graham Harrison [San Francisco: Ignatius Press, 1986], 81).

It is of note, furthermore, that adherents of all authentic rites (primitive, as in PNG or Africa, or sophisticated, as in Shintoism) claim a divine or quasi-divine (mythical) origin for their rituals.[13] It is this sacred nature of the ritual that binds its practitioners to reenact the ceremony in strict adherence to the rituals handed down by their specific tradition. Sacred rites are, by that very definition, simply not at the disposal of those who conduct them or participate in them. One can hardly expect the natives of Amazonia to take any Christian liturgy seriously that is the result of experimentation[14] or has been drawn up by a committee of experts, even if the experts are themselves natives of Amazonia. Such an approach offends against the basic principle of Christian liturgy, namely, that it is "not made by man but is gifted by God".[15] In this context, one might recall Ratzinger's comment:

> Evangelization is not simply adaptation to the culture, either, nor is it dressing up the gospel with elements of the culture, along the lines of a superficial notion of inculturation that supposes that, with modified figures of speech

[13] The same principle is found for the Old Testament rituals; see, for example, how the rituals for the sacred ordination of Aaron and his sons were carried out "as the Lord commissioned Moses" (Lev 8:13, 17, 21, 29, 36). This was noted by Pius XII in his encyclical on liturgical renewal, *Mediator Dei*: "... when God institutes the Old Law, He makes provision besides for sacred rites, and determines in exact detail the rules to be observed by His people in rendering Him the worship He ordains" (16). A glance at the history of religion shows that man is not in a position to enter into relationship with God. "Positively it means that the existing means of relating to God go back to an initiative on the latter's part, the tradition of which is passed on within a community as the wisdom of the ancients" (Ratzinger, *Behold the Pierced One: An Approach to a Spiritual Christology*, trans. Graham Harrison [San Francisco: Ignatius Press, 1986], 29).

[14] Cf. *SC* 40:2.

[15] P. Anselem Günthör, O.S.B., *Papst Benedikt XVI. zu den Problemen unserer Zeit* (Kissleg: fe Mediumverlag, 2006), 50.

and a few new elements in the liturgy, the job is done.
No, the gospel is a slit, a purification that becomes maturation and healing.... It is a cut, then that requires sympathy
and understanding of the culture from within, an appreciation for its dangers and its hidden or evident potential.[16]

When I was teaching in the major seminary of Papua
New Guinea and the Solomon Islands—whose indigenous
peoples, for all their differences, bear some striking resem-
blances to those of the Amazon region—I experienced at
first hand both some of the botched efforts to "inculturate" the Roman Rite[17] as well as some striking examples

[16] Ratzinger, *On the Way to Jesus Christ*, trans. Michael J. Miller (San Francisco: Ignatius Press, 2005), 48. The "slit" is a reference to Saint Basil's met-
aphor of slitting the "figs" of the sycamore tree before they can ripen (taken
from the Septuagint translation of Amos 7:14 about the prophet as the dresser
of sycamores). "The Logos itself must slit our cultures and their fruit, so that
what is unusable is purified and becomes not only usable but good" (ibid., 47);
see also Ratzinger, *The Spirit of the Liturgy*, trans. John Saward (San Francisco:
Ignatius Press, 2000), 200–203, where he reminds us that: "In the religious
sphere, culture manifests itself above all in the growth of authentic popular
piety" (201) and points to the popular piety in Latin America as an example.
Too much emphasis has been laid on trying to force the liturgy into artificial
forms of "adaptation".

[17] This is in contrast with the approach taken by earlier missionaries with a
knowledge of patrology, such as the German Father Alfons Schaefer, S.V.D.
(1904–1958), who pioneered the Divine Word missions in the Highlands of
New Guinea in the 1930s. Faced with primitive tribes that had never been
discovered before, his attitude to their rituals was inspired by the *Letter of Pope
Saint Gregory the Great to the Abbot Mellitus* (ca. 597), when the latter was about
to join Saint Augustine of Canterbury's mission to the pagan Anglo-Saxon
tribes. The pope instructed the missionaries to transform the places of idol
worship into churches but also to retain what was human in the religious celebrations. Earlier than Saint Gregory, Saint Patrick, it seems, had adopted a
similar approach to the Celtic pagan practices with which he was familiar in
Ireland, such as the Holy Wells. In any case, the early Irish Church transformed
the pagan sanctuary on the island in Lough Derg on the border of Northern
Ireland or the (presumably pre-Celtic) Festival of Lughnasa (named after the
Celtic god Lugh) into places and times of Christian pilgrimage and harvest
feast respectively. The rituals practiced on Lough Derg (and in other places of

of how it was enriched by authentic inculturation. Leaving aside the danger of syncretism, Western missionaries often tend to be unaware of the deeper associations that elements of native rituals have (some very negative). For this reason alone, individual symbols of a culture cannot be torn from their original ritual matrix and arbitrarily incorporated into the liturgical celebration of the sacraments without distorting both the original pagan rite and the Catholic liturgy into which they have been inserted. This I witnessed in the Regional Seminary of PNG and the Solomon Islands, when I was professor there. One unfortunate example is etched into my memory. During the Easter Vigil, seminarians from New Britain used the smoke of burning coconut, simmering in a coconut shell, which had been cut in two to be opened at the Consecration, releasing the smoke as incense. This produced screams of horror from some women from that island, who happened to be in the congregation for the Easter ceremonies. They recognized the "sacred smoke" as part of the secret rituals that were reserved to men only and that women were strictly forbidden to see under dire threats. They rushed screaming out of the chapel.

On the other hand, I attended the ordination to the priesthood of a former seminarian in a remote village on the island of Guadalcanal, Solomon Islands, which was an inspiring example of authentic inculturation. The young candidate for ordination arrived in his native attire—mostly

pilgrimage, such as Guadalupe) have been studied by Victor Turner and Edith Turner in their book: *Image and Pilgrimage in Christian Culture: Anthropological Perspectives* (Oxford: Basil Blackwell, 1978). Those ritual dynamics follow the same pattern as those to be found in primitive tribal rites. On the Holy Wells, see Philipp Rosemann's article "The Holy Wells", *The Furrow* 71 (2020): 131– 36; 195–201. On the influence of pagan religious festivals on the origins of the feasts of Christmas and Epiphany, see Johannes Roldanus, *The Church in the Age of Constantine: The Theological Challenges* (London and New York: Routledge, 2006), 168–70.

precious shells and colorful plumage of exotic tropical birds—
accompanied by his parents. At the entrance, they removed
the plumage and clothed him in a white soutane, the initial
symbol of passing over from one state of life to another.
But, apart from the laying-on of hands in silence, the most
electrifying part of the beautiful celebration (mostly sung)
was the singing of the Litany of the Saints, during which
the ordinand in his white alb lay outstretched, face down,
before the altar. That evening, I spoke with the choirmaster
and told him how moved I had been by the Litany. The
music for the Litany of the Saints, which he had composed,
he informed me, was inspired by that used in their local
burial ceremony when the dead person, wrapped in white,
was carried from where he died to the grave. The singing
resonated with the faithful's own primordial human experiences.[18] From the heightened atmosphere in the church
during the Litany, it was obvious that the profound existential significance of the ordination as a passing over from
one state of life to another was sensed by all present. That is
enculturated liturgy!

   Joseph Ratzinger's contribution (1964–1965) to the
subcommission charged with drafting the council's Decree
on Missionary Activity (*Ad Gentes*) is worth recalling in
this context. He wrote:

> The cultural and religious values of the nations are not sim-
> ply natural values which precede the Gospel and as such
> are simply added to it. Such an outlook ascribes to such
> values both too much and too little. In this world of ours,
> nature and the supernatural are never strictly separated but
> they penetrate each other. Because of this, all truly human
> values are marked both by a divine supernatural elevation
> and by human sin. They can never be simply added to the

---

[18] The composer, I was told, was illiterate but had developed an ear for
music—and he was evidently imbued with the *sensus fidei*.

Gospel, but they serve the Gospel in accord with the law of the cross and resurrection. Pagan religion dies in Christian faith, but in the same faith human religion rises and offers to faith the forms in which faith then in different ways articulates itself.[19]

Fifty years later, in his address to the students of the Urbaniana University of Rome (October 21, 2014), Pope Emeritus Benedict XVI wrote specifically with regard to the Church's mission to tribal religions:

> The encounter with [Jesus Christ] is not a barging in of a stranger that destroys their own culture and their own history. It is instead the entrance to something greater, towards which they are journeying. Consequently this encounter is always at the same time a purification and a maturation. Furthermore, the encounter is always reciprocal. Christ waits on their history, their wisdom, the way they see things.

That theological vision based on purification and maturation is, it seems to me, urgently needed to counter the seriously misleading approach to the primordial cultures and rites of the autochthonous natives of Amazonia (and indeed the more remote parts of Africa) to be found in the *Final Document* of the Synod on the Amazon. Its approach is basically that of modern Western rationalism and so is inherently alien to the Amazonian ritual practices and their existential dynamics. And that approach is equally alien to the dynamics of the Church's ancient yet ever new divine liturgy.

---

[19] The original German text is reproduced in *JRGS*, 7/1, 230–1; see Jaren Wicks' English translation, "Six Texts by Prof. Joseph Ratzinger as *peritus* before and during Vatican Council II", *Gregorianum* 89 (2008): 289.

Chapter Six

A NEW LITURGY FOR
A NEW EPOCH

In the era of a Catholicism that is truly global and thus truly catholic, [the Church] must ever more adjust to the fact that not all laws can be applied to each land in the same way, that, above all, the liturgy must be like a mirror of the unity as also an appropriate expression of the respective spiritual particularity [of each nation].

—Joseph Ratzinger, Cardinal Frings
Genoese speech, 1961[1]

The French Church historian Henri Daniel-Rops once pointed out that the Second Vatican Council was unique insofar as it was not called to overcome any crisis, as was the case in all previous general councils. He cited the then-Cardinal Montini and future Pope Paul VI: "Unlike many

[1] Peter Seewald, *Benedikt XVI: Ein Leben* (Munich: Droemer, 2020), 384. To recap, in the Genoese speech he wrote for Cardinal Frings in 1961 outlining his vision for the council (see introduction, note 1 above), Ratzinger described the social changes in the world since the Second World War as characterized by three phenomena: globalization, reliance on technology, and scientism. Within that context, he argued that the Church, in dialogue with modernity, must present the Christian faith as a liveable alternative worthy of living. The Church, as people gathered from the nations, must take into consideration the multiform nature of human life.

other councils, Vatican II is convening at a peaceful, religiously zealous moment in the life of the Church."[2] It would be a pastoral council to promote the renewal of the Church in the whole world. Almost three thousand bishops attended; it was the biggest general council ever held.[3] While the council was in session, there was a sense that something exceptional was happening in Rome—that it marked the end of an era. To some, it was the end of the post-Tridentine era, while to others it was the end of the Constantinian era. To this writer, it seems that, more precisely, Vatican II marked the end of that epoch in Church history marked by the break between the Greek and Latin forms of post-Constantinian Christian civilizations, when in the eleventh century the West and the East finally parted ways in what is known as the Great Schism of 1054. In the East, the highly developed Byzantium civilization faced the challenge of the rise of Islam, while, in the West, the Latin Christian civilization of the second millennium emerged from the reforms of Pope Gregory VII (Hildebrand, who died in 1085).

Allowing the liturgy to be celebrated in the vernacular of the local Churches was, in effect, the announcement of a new epoch in the Church's history: the end of an exclusively Latin Christianity that had developed in the West. Historians in the future may well see Vatican II as the beginning of a new flowering of the catholicity of the Church—her universal nature—as made up of believers of every nation, tribe, people, and tongue (Rev 7:9; see also

[2] Quoted in Ratzinger, "Ten Years after the Beginning of the Council", in *Dogma and Preaching: Applying Christian Doctrine to Daily Life*, ed. Michael J. Miller (San Francisco: Ignatius Press, 2011), 377.

[3] Given the sheer logistical difficulty of conducting one of that size, it is doubtful if there will ever be another such general council, though modern technology might make it possible.

5:9) under the heavens. In many ways, it is such, thanks largely to the extraordinary missionary achievements of the post-Tridentine Church over the previous four hundred years.[4] The explicitly "ecumenical" nature of the council—reaching out to all the Christian Churches and ecclesial communions that had been separated for centuries but especially since the break with the East in the eleventh century—was experienced at the time as an attempt to recover the Church's truly universal nature. After the schism with Byzantium, the Church's authentic Catholicity (her universal or inclusive nature) had taken on an increasingly exclusive meaning, initially vis-à-vis the Orthodox Churches. In the wake of the Reformation, the term Catholic took on an ever more narrow, sectarian meaning,[5] without ever losing its universal claim or self-consciousness. Paradoxically, it was the pre-Vatican II experience of a familiar rite, while attending Mass in Latin in whatever country of the globe one found oneself, that expressed the true catholicity or universality of the Church.

In the foreword to the double volume of his *Collected Writings* devoted to his publications on Vatican II,[6] Pope Benedict XVI recalled the council's opening ceremony on October 11, 1962, and how impressed he was "to see in

[4] It should be noted that emigration caused by various political, economic, and historical events (such as wars and colonialism) also contributed to the spread of the Church. This is also true of the Orthodox Churches, which are local and ethnic by nature, but which in the last two centuries have spread throughout the world mostly through emigration. In the wake of the colonial conquests, the various Anglican and Protestant missionary movements originating in the European imperial power bases likewise made these ecclesial communities more universal.

[5] In a sense, it culminated in the civil war in Northern Ireland (euphemistically known as "The Troubles") between "Catholics" and "Protestants" that first erupted in that fateful year: 1968.

[6] English translation: https://www.archivioradiovaticana.va/storico/2012/10/10/pope_pens_rare_article_on_his_inside_view_of_vatican_ii/en1–628717.

the entrance procession bishops from all over the world, from all peoples and all races: an image of the Church of Jesus Christ which embraces the whole world, in which the peoples of the earth know they are united in his peace." And he adds: "It was a moment of great expectation." There was a sense that nothing less than the future of Christianity—and so, of mankind—was somehow or other at stake: "Christianity, which had built and formed the Western world, seemed more and more to be losing its power to shape society. It appeared weary and it looked as if the future would be determined by other spiritual forces. The sense of this loss of the present on the part of Christianity, and of the task following on from that, was well summed up in the word 'aggiornamento' (updating). Christianity must be in the present if it is to be able to form the future."

As mentioned above, it was only in the course of its deliberations that, as Pope Paul VI indicated in a homily at the closure of the council, its true significance became evident. Because of the predominant forgetfulness of God today in the West—now truly "a secular age" (Charles Taylor)—the question of God became central. And that, it seems to me, is the key to understanding the true nature of the postconciliar crisis. It could be described as the Church's ongoing, herculean struggle to come to terms with a radically new world view forged in the epicenter of what is left of Western civilization unmoored from its Christian roots. And it is here that the centrality of the liturgy to Church's divine mission must be seen.

We are living through a period of historical change that is not unlike the radical change in the Church's relation to society, and so to mankind at large, that was inaugurated by Constantine's embrace of the Christian religion in the fourth century; indeed, it may well be seen by future historians to have been even more momentous.

The underlying theological—and thus liturgical—issues are even more threatening to the nature and mission of the Church than the Arian crisis or the new Church-State relations that marked the fourth century: what is at stake today is nothing less than the theoretical, and widespread, practical denial of the existence of God.

In completing what was left unfinished by the First Vatican Council, the Second Vatican Council was initially concerned with redefining the Church's own nature with the aim of reigniting the zeal needed for her mission to save mankind. In recovering a broader view of Church as founded in Scripture, the Fathers, and tradition, Vatican II aimed to overcome the narrow self-understanding of Church as a *societas perfecta* that had emerged in the post-Reformation period with regard to the relationship of Church and State.[7] It was a view of the Church understood primarily as an institution parallel to the State, while, at the same time, transcending it. The Church, which saw herself as the real "perfect society", had come to define herself vis-à-vis the State.

What was needed was a new understanding of the Church.

Shortly before he took up his first academic post as lecturer in the Archdiocese of Munich's Major Seminary in Freising, Joseph Ratzinger read two papers at the Austrian Week for Theologians held in Salzburg from July 14 to 20, 1958.[8] The topic of the first paper was the "Church

---

[7] As Father Dermot Fenlon reminded me, the Church as perfect society does not mean the realized perfection of her members, but only that she has all the means of perfection in the sacraments. Nonetheless, because of the Church-State tensions that almost define the post-Reformation period, the use of the term tended to promote the self-consciousness of the Church as an institution parallel to the State.

[8] Published for the first time in *Mitteilungen des Institut Papst Benedikt XVI*, no. 1, ed. Rudolf Voderholzer, Christian Schaller, and Franz-Xavier Heibl (Regensburg: Schnell & Steiner, 2008), 13–49.

and Liturgy".[9] It provides us with a unique insight into Ratzinger's nascent understanding of the Church and the central role of the liturgy in it. It should be noted that it was some six months before Pope Saint John XXIII convoked the Second Vatican Council. Arguing from Scripture, Ratzinger claimed that the Church is best understood, *not* as a "perfect society" on the model of the State, but as the living Body of Christ in history. In other words, the Church, understood as a living organism, the Body of Christ. The Church is mankind's place of worship (*die Kultstätte der Menschheit*). She is "the new Temple, which God himself has built up in mankind as *naos acheiropoiētos* [a Temple not built by human hands]. Consequently: if it is of the essence of the Church to be *Christus Totus*, the ever-present Body of Christ in history, then it is also essential to her, by that very means and to that extent, that she [will] be the true Temple in the world, the living place of worship in time."[10] This establishes the profound significance of the divine liturgy for the Church.

> If therefore, for the Jews, Temple and ancient Passover [rituals] are the *fons unitatis*—source of the nation's existence—the Church likewise exists solely on the basis of the Passover of the death of Christ and His being ever-present in the liturgy of the Church. She experiences in

[9] "Kirche und Liturgie", in ibid., 13–27; the second paper is entitled "Was ist der Mensch?", an initial sketch of what would become his theological anthropology.

[10] "Kirche und Liturgie", 14–15. He outlines the NT account of Christ's relationship to the Temple, beginning with his symbolic action known as the purification of the Temple, which is to be understood as a prophetic anticipation of his own death and Resurrection (cf. Jn 2:19); this interpretation is confirmed by Mark 14:58: "I will destroy this temple that is made with hands [*ton naon touton ton cheiropoiētos*], and in three days I will build another, not made with hands [*acheiropoiētos*]." The Body of Christ—the Church—is the new place of worship in the world of men.

her cult that creative happening, out of which alone can she exist continually as Church. She exists as People of God, not on account of the fact that she has the organizational institutions of a *societas perfecta*, but rather solely on account of the fact that her true divine source of life flows from the cult. This is because in the cult she continually experiences her new foundation arising from the life-giving powers of God, from the divine-human salvific act of Jesus Christ.[11]

All the institutions of the Church—Primacy, episcopacy, priesthood—have constitutive significance only insofar as they are essentially interwoven with her sacramental organism and can only be understood from their cultic source of life. "The existence of the Church as Church depends on the cult, which in the liturgy finds its concrete form."[12]

The term "cult" as used here by Ratzinger connotes more than ritual; it embraces that fuller understanding of worship which defines Christian living, namely, the daily sacrifice of doing God's will that is ritually expressed in and empowered by the divine liturgy. Ratzinger unfolds the implications of this for a deeper and broader understanding of the liturgy as a vibrant reality that extends way beyond the church doors into the darkest depths of the suffering Church. "In her martyrs, she carries the death

[11] Ibid., 18.

[12] Ibid., 19. Ratzinger's thought could be summed up as follows in the words of Fagerberg: "[L]iturgy [is] foundational to Christian identity. 'To swim' is a verb, 'swimmer' is the noun. Liturgy is the verb form of 'Church' and 'Church' is the noun form of 'liturgy'" (David W. Fagerberg, *On Liturgical Asceticism* [Washington, D.C.: Catholic University of America, 2013], 1), even though Fagerberg does not refer to Ratzinger's writing in this important study. I am grateful to Andrew T. J. Kaethler for introducing me to the work of Fagerberg, but it was too late to do justice to his rich and provocative writings. See also Corbon, *The Wellsprings of Worship*; Kavanagh, *On Liturgical Theology*.

of the Lord perpetually in her Body, and in the suffering
of her members, further, she suffers perpetually [in union
with] the suffering of the Lord: the suffering of her own
[faithful] is a truly liturgical service: a continuation of the
saving Passion of the Lord. There is no boundary between
liturgy and life."[13] Ratzinger would develop this theme
above all in his paper "Eucharist and Mission" (1997),[14]
where he interprets Saint Paul's description of his own
expected martyrdom in liturgical terms: "Even if I am to
be poured out as a libation upon the sacrificial offering of
your faith, I am glad" (Phil 2:17). The apostle views his
pending death as being liturgical in character since his life
is being spilled out as a sacrificial gift for others.[15]

> What happens in this is a becoming one with the self-
> giving of Jesus Christ, with his great act of love, which
> is as such the true worship of God.... It is worship being
> lived out in life, which is recognized as such by faith,
> and thus it is serving faith. Because this is true liturgy, it
> achieves the end to which all liturgy is directed: joy—that
> joy which can arise only from the encounter between man
> and God, from the removal of the barriers and limitations
> of earthly existence.[16]

What Paul expresses in a single short sentence is fully
developed in the account of the martyrdom of Saint
Polycarp and is found in a more popular form in the

---

[13] Ratzinger, "Kirche und Liturgie", 20. Re Ratzinger's notion of "cult",
see his *Volk Gottes und Haus Gottes in Augustin's Lehre von der Kirche* (St. Ottilien: EOS Verlag, 1992), 188ff.

[14] In Ratzinger, *Pilgrim Fellowship of Faith*, trans. by Henry Taylor (San Francisco: Ignatius Press, 2005), 90–122; see esp. 111–14.

[15] Ratzinger refers to P. Bonnard, "Mourir et vivre avec Jésus-Christ selon
Saint Paul", *Rev. d'histoire et de philosophie religieuse* 36 (1956): 101–12.

[16] *Pilgrim Fellowship of Faith*, 112.

account of Saint Lawrence's martyrdom.[17] In sum, "We might ... understand the Eucharist as being (if the term is correctly understood) the mystical heart of Christianity, in which God mysteriously comes forth, time and again, from within himself and draws us into his embrace."[18]

૨૦ ૨૦ ૨૦

In 1970, five years after the end of the council, Ratzinger asked the question: How will the Church look in the year 2000?[19] Due in no small measure to the cultural upheaval of the later 1960s, the initial euphoria had given way to conflict. The cracks between the preconciliar progressive theologians began to surface together, at the other end of the spectrum, with a hardening of divisions among the conservative currents of thought. All these divisions had first emerged during the council's own deliberations (especially on *Schema XIII*, which became *Gaudium et Spes*). The more radical progressive theologians became the dominant force for change after the council in an era that was characterized by the abandonment of Being for Becoming, i.e., the abandonment of metaphysics for a future-oriented historical process.[20] This led to the predominant, neo-Marxist, cultural imperative to change society in order to

[17] Ibid., 112–14.

[18] Ratzinger, "Eucharist and Mission", in *Pilgrim Fellowship of Faith*, 121.

[19] "What Will the Future Church Look Like?" in Ratzinger, *Faith and the Future* (San Francisco: Ignatius Press, 2009), 101–18.

[20] Ratzinger gives a comprehensive account of the various theological currents in his essay: "Ten Years after the Beginning of the Council—Where Do We Stand?", in *Dogma and Preaching*, 377–84. The most profound reason for embracing change he attributes to abandoning metaphysics and replacing it with neo-Marxist progressivism. Through the influence of Ernst Bloch, the Christian notion of hope was transmogrified into political theology with utopian goals for the future of the world. See also Peter Seewald, *Benedikt XVI. Ein Leben* (Munich: Droemer, 2020), 555ff.

create a better future, an imperative that found its most
extreme expression in the 1968 student revolts.[21] Change
became the dominant imperative also in the Church—
change even in her moral teaching.[22] The reformed
liturgy—the Ordinary Form of the Roman Rite, or, more
colloquially, the Mass in the vernacular, had, generally
speaking, a profoundly unsettling effect on Catholics who,
like myself, had been brought up to consider every detail
of the Mass to be sacred and, thus, literally untouchable.[23]
The future was on everyone's mind—the progressives full
of optimism, the conservatives full of pessimism—while
the original proponents of renewal, who were inspired by
a fuller Catholic tradition,[24] were sidelined. And the actual
texts of Vatican II were forgotten. What, indeed, would
the future look like?

Ratzinger warned his readers to be wary of easy progno-
ses. Church history is full of unexpected events, he wrote,
such as those periods in recent history, like the situation of
the Church in the wake of the French Revolution, when
it seemed that the Church was on the point of extinction,

---

[21] Cf. Twomey, "May 1968", *Verbum SVD*, 59 (2018): 104–17.

[22] This is the deepest reason why the publication of *Humanae Vitae* in 1968,
which reiterated the Church's teaching on marriage and sexuality, was rejected
even by theologians and bishops; cf. Twomey, *Moral Theology after* Humanae
Vitae (Dublin: Four Courts Press, 2010).

[23] Writing to the German bishops on April 14, 2012, about the translation of
pro multis, Pope Benedict XVI commented: "We all know from [the] experience of the last fifty years how deeply the alteration of liturgical forms and texts
touches people's souls."

[24] Ratzinger would presumably include himself and others, such as Hans Urs
von Balthasar and Henri de Lubac, among the third current of postconciliar
thought; they were among the instigators of the International Catholic Review
Communio, which was founded to offset the quarterly *Concilium*, the voice of
the mainstream progressive theologies; see Tracey Rowland, *Catholic Theology*
(London: Bloomsbury, 2017), on the *Communio* approach to theology (91–137)
and on the *Concilium* approach (139–66).

only to be reborn and flourish with new vitality in the following century. And yet, we can learn from history if we want to overcome the blindness of the present moment. That is the main point that G. K. Chesterton made with typical eloquence and insight when he wrote: "Christendom has had a series of revolutions and in each one of them Christianity has died. Christianity has died many times and risen again; for it had a God who knew the way out of the grave."[25]

Applying the lessons learned from those historical periods that in some way, *mutatis mutandis*, reflect the situation we face in the post-Vatican-II Church, Ratzinger claims that:

> The future of the Church can and will issue from those whose roots are deep and who live from the pure fullness of their faith. It will not issue from those who accommodate themselves merely to the passing moment.... The future of the Church, once again as always, will be reshaped by saints, by men, that is, whose minds probe deeper than the slogans of the day, who see more than others see, because their lives embrace a wider reality. Unselfishness, which makes men free, is attained only through the patience of small, daily acts of self-denial.[26]

In this way, bit by bit, they open their hearts to God. This applies in particular to the priest, who is called to be more than a social worker (however important that may be). Animated by God, he must reach out to people in their sorrows, their joys, their hopes, and in their anxiety.

---

[25] G. K. Chesterton, *The Everlasting Man*, first published in 1929 (San Francisco: Ignatius Press, 1993), 250. The final chapter, entitled "The Five Deaths of the Faith", should be compulsory reading for committed but anxious Christians today.

[26] Ratzinger, *Faith and the Future*, 114.

Such a priest will always be indispensable.[27] The Church
of the future will be small, one that has been deprived of
her social status and privileges, but also one that will rely
more on the initiatives of her individual members.[28] With
all the changes that must of necessity take place and will be
time-consuming and laborious, the Church will eventually
rediscover her true essence: "faith in the triune God, in
Jesus Christ, the Son of God made man, in the presence
of the Spirit until the end of the world. In faith and prayer
she will again recognize her true center and experience the
sacraments again as the worship of God and not as a subject
for liturgical scholarship."[29]

What did Ratzinger mean when he said that the Church
in the future would be defined by an authentic *experience*
of the sacraments as worship of God? Was he referring to
authentic *participatio actuosa* more or less along the lines
I have tried to outline above? The term "experience"
might be slightly off-putting for more traditional theologians and liturgists alike. We should not underestimate
the still prevalent influence on our thinking of the Neoscholastic mindset in general and, even more so, the dominant rationalistic mentality of the technological age that

[27] Ratzinger foresaw the possible ordination of part-time priests, without
in any way dispensing with the need for the full-time priest. He does not use
the term *viri probati*, but his description matches the notion. Three years later,
he seems to have changed his mind; see "Where Do We Stand?", *Dogma and
Preaching*, 383, where he scathingly refers to the demand for a "functional"
ministry. In his recent publication together with Robert Cardinal Sarah,
*From the Depths of Our Hearts: Priesthood, Celibacy, and the Crisis of the Cath-
olic Church*, trans. Michael J. Miller (San Francisco: Ignatius Press, 2020), he
only alludes once, without comment, to the practice of married clerics in the
Orthodox traditions. Otherwise, he provides a profound theology and spirituality of the priesthood demonstrating how celibacy is intrinsically related to
Christian priesthood.

[28] Cf. "Die neue Heiden und der Kirche", *Hochland* 51 (1958/59): 1–11.

[29] Ratzinger, *Glaube und Vernunft*, 117.

shuns experience as too "subjective".[30] As I tried to indicate above, liturgy is primarily about an intensely personal participation in the communal or, better, ecclesial
worship of God—a grace-endowed, ritual experience—
that corresponds to (but transcends) those dynamics that
constitute authentic ritual, dynamics that are built into
our embodied human nature. Experience is not something that is sought after for its own sake. That would
reduce liturgy to a form of entertainment. Neither is it to
be identified with what might be called a mystical experience of the Real Presence.[31]

But it must be frankly admitted that the present ritual of the Ordinary Form has certain inherent weaknesses
that, unless they are overcome, could work against the
kind of ritual experience that should be expected when
celebrating the sacraments, especially, but not only, the
Mass. And they have to be overcome, since, for the majority of the faithful and clerics, the Ordinary Form of
the Roman Rite is quite literally for them the ordinary
form of the Mass: it is the rite with which they are most
familiar—and, from the point of view of ritual, it is of
supreme importance. Though ritually impoverished as
compared with the Extraordinary Form, the "new Mass"
has the potential for genuine liturgical expression, as has
been demonstrated in the diverse cultures around the
world, provided the needed embellishments of the Ordinary Form are not imposed by a committee of experts but
are allowed to develop organically in time. This can be

[30] Indeed, among us aging clerics of the 1968-era (both liberal and conservative), the vestiges of the legalistic attitude to liturgy are still evident in our
minimalistic approach to the liturgy, which likewise mitigates against any stress
on an authentic ritual experience.

[31] An experience that is described by Mrs. Alison Wilson: *Before & After*
(London: Constable, 2019), 81–88.

expected to happen, as it has in part already happened, in Africa and Asia, where the people's own natural ritual instincts have not been significantly dulled by the rationalism and functionalism of modernity.

❧ ❧ ❧

The first time I appreciated the ritual potential of the Ordinary Form of the Mass was in the magnificent neo-Romanesque-Byzantine-style Basilica of Sacré-Coeur, Montmartre, Paris, when I was on my way overland to a German-language course in the Bavarian Alps in 1969. Celebrated under the gaze of Christ in Glory depicted in a mosaic in the apse, the solemn liturgy of the Sunday Mass was simple, beautiful, full of light, rich in movement, gestures, and silences, but also embedded as well in modern but sublime polyphonic music that embraced the voice of the community in harmony.

Some five decades later, I experienced the potential of the Ordinary Form of the Roman Rite in a very different setting (in Ireland), which brought home to me how, despite initial clumsiness, the new ritual had on the whole matured well. This was the Requiem Mass for my first-cousin's widowed wife in her own parish church (of no great architectural merit from the late 1950s) in a working-class district of Cork City. A mother of five and a daily Mass-goer most of her life, she had also been a Eucharistic minister and so was familiar with the liturgy. Before dementia set in, she herself had chosen the hymns—and had chosen them well. She left clear instructions about some of the details of the liturgy (e.g., the readings; only her rosary and favorite prayer book should be included in the Offertory procession), and she insisted that there be no eulogy! One of her sons, a senior police officer (whose inbuilt sense of ritual had evidently been fine-tuned through police ceremonials) organized the Funeral Mass according to her instructions and within the shortest time possible (two days before Christmas). He trained the readers (her children and grandchildren), specified their movements to and from the altar with almost military precision, and entrusted the hymns and music to an ensemble of three Irish traditional musicians. The Requiem was truly uplifting, marked as it was by familiarity, noble simplicity, and humble dignity—with the emotions held in check by an undercurrent of sacral reverence.

I have experienced on various occasions in different parts of the world the potential of the Ordinary Form of the Roman Rite to be sublime in an even more exalted sense, such as at the Ordination to the Priesthood in the Solomon Islands of a former student, as mentioned above, but also at the Episcopal Ordination of Christoph von Schönborn in the Cathedral of Saint Stephan, Vienna, and, unforgettably, at the Solemn Mass on the occasion of Cardinal Ratzinger's golden jubilee as a priest in one of the oldest churches in Rome, the Basilica of Santa Maria in Trastevere. But I also experienced it while participating in the Holy Week ceremonies in the stunningly beautiful neo-Gothic seminary chapel of Saint Patrick's College, Maynooth. The college's long tradition of sacred music and the seminarians' familiarity with Scripture lifted the liturgy on this occasion into the realm of the sublime.

There is another, humbler potential of the Ordinary Rite that needs to be acknowledged, i.e., the capacity of the rite to be celebrated in those places outside the normal liturgical space, such as Mass celebrated in bush-mission stations or during summer youth camps, though here special attention must be paid to observing the rubrics and creating a temporary "sacred space".[32] The Ordinary Form is thus flexible—perhaps too flexible—but its evident drawback (the temptation to engage in unwarranted creativity) can be overcome, once one is aware of the dangers inherent in it. Such situations demand especially from the priest a certain self-discipline and the acquisition of an authentic *ars celebrandi* so that his own personality does not impinge on his role as acting *in persona Christi*.[33]

The Ordinary Form of the Mass demands more attention be given to the *ars celebrandi* than is the case with the Extraordinary Form, though it applies to both. In short, Mass celebrated by a Padre Pio is evidently more "effective" than a Mass said by a cleric anxious to release his congregation as quickly and painlessly as possible. This is so, even though both Masses are equally effective *ex opere operato* with regard to the mystery of sacrifice of the Mass. But what a difference the *ars celebrandi* makes, i.e., *ex opere operantis*!

However, there is also the downside of familiarity. According to Pope Benedict XVI,

> when we continually encounter the sacred, it risks becoming habitual for us. In this way, reverential fear is

[32] Saying Mass *ad orientem* in such situations (with proper catechesis beforehand) would automatically create such a sacred space and retain the cosmic dimension of the liturgy.

[33] One such situation remains etched in my memory; it was the celebration of the sacraments of reconciliation and the Eucharist in a bush-prison in Kundiawa, in the Highlands of Papua New Guinea, while doing supply work during a vacation from the seminary. Dressed in a simple soutane and stole and sitting on an upturned bucket outside the jail's latrine, I "heard" the confessions of the prisoners before "saying" a simple Mass in the *hausman* (men's dormitory), constructed of bush material (the dormitory traditionally used by men in PNG). The altar was the case of the Mass-kit placed on the bamboo platform in the *hausman* used for sleeping. God was there: that is all that mattered. Jesus Christ, true God and true man, was present and active, abolishing all human divisions, transcending our lowly circumstances, and reaching into the depths of our hearts.

extinguished. Conditioned by all our habits, we no longer perceive the great, new and surpassing fact that he himself is present, speaks to us, gives himself to us. We must ceaselessly struggle against this becoming accustomed to the extraordinary reality, against the indifference of the heart, always recognizing our insufficiency anew and the grace that there is in the fact that he consigned himself to our hands. To serve means to draw near, but above all it means obedience.[34]

An essential part of the ritual for the so-called Tridentine Mass included the observance of silence in the sacristy while the priest vested, silently reciting short prayers to accompany each item of his liturgical vestments. In this way, he was reminded of the awesome ritual he was about to enter as he approached the sanctuary. (It is still practised by those who celebrate the Extraordinary Form of the Mass.) The time might be ripe to reintroduce them to the Ordinary Rite, since the ritual of the Mass actually begins in the sacristy.[35]

❧ ❧ ❧

However, familiarity, as Pope Benedict XVI noted, can also breed indifference. All authentic ritual, Victor Turner stresses, includes regular changes (solemnities, feasts, memorials, etc.) and even interruptions—such as one day in the year when no Mass is celebrated (Good Friday)— provided they, too, are included in a broader agreed-upon

[34] *Homily for the Chrism Mass*, Holy Thursday, March 20, 2008, in Saint Peter's Basilica, as quoted in Ratzinger and Robert Cardinal Sarah, *From the Depths of Our Hearts*, 54–55.

[35] In many churches, the practice has developed whereby priest, extraordinary ministers and servers recite together a short prayer before and after Mass. That is clearly a step in the right direction. Unfortunately, the prayers themselves tend to be rather banal, indeed, moralizing in tone.

rhythm. Understood in this way, the (limited) discretion allowed to the celebrant in the new Roman Missal with regard to the occasional changes of detail (penitential rites, etc.) can be seen in a more positive light, provided the limits set down in the rubrics are kept. What the dynamics of ritual clearly exclude is the priest taking it on himself arbitrarily to introduce entirely novel features into the celebration of the sacraments purely on his own initiative. This is what Ratzinger described as "flirting with self-concocted liturgies".[36] It is also what the council expressly forbade (cf. SC 22). The cleric, too, must be prepared to submit to what is given in all its details, to what the Church has sanctioned in the approved rituals, in the spirit of "not my will, but yours, be done" (Lk 22:42). In ritual, every detail is important, every word, moment of silence, gesture (kneeling, standing, folded hands, extended hands), every item (not only bread and wine, but also altar, altar clothes, number of candles, vestments, altar linen, missal, lectionary, bells, thurifer, incense, processional cross, etc.) is dense with symbolic meaning.[37] Attention to these details is paramount, details whose rich meaning is a given and is there to be rediscovered; they are the product of ritual experience stretching back millennia beyond the Old Testament and into the primordial rituals of mankind, as, for example, incense, fire, and the flickering flame of candles. They cannot be arbitrarily invented by the celebrant. Their "givenness" (rooted in tradition) is what enriches every liturgy and creates the sense of the sacred without artificiality or effort.[38]

[36] Ratzinger, "Where Do We Stand?", Dogma and Preaching, 382.

[37] See the chapter entitled "The Body and Liturgy", in Ratzinger, Spirit of the Liturgy, 171–224.

[38] Chesterton once remarked that he did not know what a bishop's mitre was meant to symbolize, only that it was not simply a decoration and had some theological meaning, of which he was unaware, and that sufficed for him. I was

This inner attitude of obedience is of the essence of priestly spirituality, as Pope Benedict XVI once pointed out: "Our obedience is a believing with the Church, a thinking and speaking with the Church, serving through her. What Jesus predicted to Peter also always applies: 'You will be taken where you do not want to go.' This letting oneself be guided where one does not want to be led is an essential dimension of our [priestly] service, and it is exactly what make us free. In this being guided, which can be contrary to our ideas and plans, we experience something new—the wealth of God's love."[39] The pope at that stage in his homily was not referring explicitly to obedience to the rubrics of the Sacramentary, but the same basic attitude, it seems to me, applies to them. Priests are servants, not masters, of what the Church prescribes. Such an attitude brings with it a certain detachment and its own inner peace. Further, commenting earlier on the term "to serve" (as found in the Second Eucharistic Prayer immediately after the Consecration), Benedict remarks:

What the priest does at that moment, in the Eucharistic celebration, is to serve God and men. The cult that Christ rendered to the Father was the giving of himself to the end for humanity. Into this cult, this service, the priest must insert himself. Thus, the word "serve" contains many dimensions. In the first place, part of it is certainly the

---

also baffled. It was only at the episcopal consecration of Joseph Ratzinger as archbishop of Munich and Freising that I discovered the meaning. The newly ordained archbishop explained the significance of the mitre when he referred to the rubric of holding the Book of the Gospels over the head of the ordinand at one stage of the ceremony: the two "peaks" of the mitre represent the Old and New Testament, which the bishop was commissioned to interpret in the light of Christ (the two natures of Christ being symbolized by the two lappets rimmed with a fringe [infulae] hanging down from the back).

[39] Homily for the Chrism Mass, Holy Thursday, March 20, 2008, in Saint Peter's Basilica, as quoted in From the Depths of Our Hearts, 56.

correct celebration of the liturgy and of the sacraments in general, accomplished though interior participation. We must learn to understand increasingly the sacred liturgy in all its essence, to develop a living familiarity with it, so that it becomes the soul of our daily life. It is then that we celebrate in the correct way; it is then that the *ars celebrandi*, the art of celebrating, emerges by itself. In this art there must be nothing artificial.[40]

Sacred liturgy should enable all worshippers to experience something of the transcendent joy of God's presence, an experience that can at times be sublime.[41]

ॐ ॐ ॐ

As Pope Benedict XVI, Joseph Ratzinger took the momentous decision to issue the 2007 *Motu Proprio* entitled *Summorum Pontificum*, permitting the general use of the so-called Tridentine Mass. This he did following the requests of the faithful who "continued to be attached

[40] Ibid., 54. The arbitrary introduction into the liturgy of what is artificial can only be described as a new form of clericalism, indeed, almost a form of terrorism, with the faithful at the mercy of the main celebrant and what he might come up with next. As entertainment, the unexpected might work, but as worship, it is alienating for the faithful who came to adore God present in their midst.

[41] Here one cannot but recall the experience of the envoys of the prince of the Russian Kiev, when they entered the Hagia Sophia in Constantinople during the divine liturgy: they did not know if they were in heaven or on earth. Otto von Simson mentions the "awesomeness" experienced by King Henry I at the consecration of Canterbury Cathedral and by Abbot Suger at the consecration of his own Abbey of Saint Denis, Paris (*The Gothic Cathedral* [Princeton, N.J.: Princeton University Press, 1989], xviii–xix). One of the greatest liturgical "experiences" with the Ordinary Rite I have had (and they are many) was the Mass for the inauguration of Pope Benedict XVI as Bishop of Rome, which the film director Zeffirelli afterward praised for its superb "choreography", as he put it. But it was more than just choreography; it was Sacred Liturgy at its best.

with such love and affection to the earlier liturgical forms which had deeply shaped their culture and spirit." He expressed the view that: "These two expressions of the Church's *lex orandi* will in no way lead to a division in the Church's *lex credendi* (rule of faith); for they are two usages of the one Roman rite." This desire to avoid division, to promote unity among believers, has ever been his primary motivation. Regretfully, it would seem that the admittedly impoverished ritual dynamics of the Ordinary Form of the Roman Rite (and, especially, their misuse by "creative" clerics) as compared to the rich ritual dynamics of the Extraordinary Form has in practice seen such a division emerge. And this is tragic, for several reasons, the most important being the way the very mission of the Church in this secular age is damaged. If the liturgy no longer serves the mission of the Church to gather together all things in Christ (cf. Eph 1:10), if it is a source of division, then something serious, indeed, is wrong, and the most perfectly conducted Extraordinary Form cannot compensate for the danger it poses to the Church's mission.

That the ritually richer Extraordinary Form (the "Latin Mass") has its own inbuilt weakness is something that is rarely admitted today by its enthusiasts. There *were* solid reasons why the Fathers of the council, in an astonishingly swift display of unanimity, called for a reform, even though they themselves had been spiritually nourished all their lives by the Tridentine Mass. In practice, as they well knew, there was considerable ritualism—casuistic/legalistic rubricism to be precise—that caused serious scrupulosity for some priests. An impoverished participation in the Mass on the part of the lay faithful had also been noted, such as attending while praying the Rosary, etc., though many would protest that they were still participating. Many accretions, some aesthetically beautiful, had been introduced in the Baroque and Rococo periods—accretions, however, that are no longer suited to the contemporary culture: in fact, they are at best theatrical; at worst, alienating. Further, slavish adherence to the rubrics can induce mere ritualism. The celebration of the Latin High Mass and Solemn Pontifical Mass can succumb to the temptation of becoming a spectacle—at times, indeed, they can be quite spectacular and very beautiful, when properly executed. Both, however, can also become a sophisticated form of entertainment for the *aficionados*, admittedly more aesthetically refined and pious, but nonetheless questionable and tending to be elitist. The pomp and circumstance of some of the accretions, however stunning, belong to a lost age. Some are, frankly, bombastic, drawing the wrong kind of attention to the presiding prelate, however humble he may be. More seriously, they can detract from the mystery of the Mass, the awesome memorial of the Passion and death of Christ. The ritual richness of the Extraordinary Form of the Roman Rite can also foster a sense of superiority—and not the required humility and gratitude that is of the essence of the celebration of the Holy Eucharist.

ﬠ ﬠ ﬠ

It was understood at the time that, by removing most of the restrictions on the use of the Latin Mass (and related rituals), Pope Benedict XVI hoped that the Ordinary Form (the Mass in the vernacular in the reformed ritual) might learn from—and so be enriched by—the preconciliar rituals. The most obvious enrichment would come from rediscovering the meaning of the orientation of both priest and people toward the east: the rising sun, symbol of Christ's return in glory anticipated in the present Eucharist. But, I suspect, that he also hoped that the adherents of the older rituals might in turn learn from the newly reformed ritual—not least in terms of its greater simplicity—by removing some of the more superfluous accretions of the ages.[42] The fact that the Extraordinary Form uses a different calendar of the liturgical year as compared with the Ordinary Form is potentially divisive in a most alarming way.

On the other hand, the use of the vernacular in the Ordinary Form must retain not only the few Hebrew and Greek terms (*Amen, allelulia, hosanna, Sabaoth, kyrie eleison*), which echo the liturgy's origins in the Old and New Testaments as well the experience of the early Church,[43] but also (at least for solemn celebrations) some of the central Latin texts of the Ordinary of the Mass (*Gloria, Credo, Sanctus, Pater Noster, Agnus Dei*), which all Catholics of every race and nation should be able to recite and chant.[44]

---

[42] As an example of the latter, one could mention the use at Solemn Pontifical Mass of special acolytes carrying candles in their hands near the Missal when the bishop, priest, or deacon should read from it. Before the invention of electricity, such candles were necessary in a darkened church. No matter what symbolic significance they may have acquired in the course of time, they are superfluous.

[43] The Welsh poet David Jones, writing long before Vatican II on the difficulties with the use of English he faced as a poet, noted how some familiar Latin phrases, such as "Requiescant in pace" or "Quicunque vult" (the so-called Athanasian Creed), evoke "exact historic over-tones and under-tones", which are lost when translated into English. In that context, he observes: "When in the Good Friday Office, the Latin, without any warning, is suddenly pierced by the Greek cry *Agios o Theos*, the Greek-speaking Roman Church of the third century becomes almost visible to us. So to juxtapose and condition the English words 'O Holy God' as to make them do what this change from Latin to Greek effects within this particular liturgical setting, would not be at all easy" (David Jones, *The Anathemata* [London and Boston: Faber and Faber, 1952; quoted from the 1972 edition's reprint, 1990], 13).

[44] In his *Motu Proprio* establishing the Pontifical Academy for Latin, *Latina Lingua* (2012), Pope Benedict XVI outlined the role played by Latin in the Church down through the centuries long after it was no longer the *lingua franca*. "In addition, precisely in order to highlight the Church's universal character, the liturgical books of the Roman Rite, the most important documents of the Papal Magisterium and the most solemn official Acts of the Roman Pontiffs are written in this language in their authentic form" (no. 2).

And this for various reasons, the most important being their symbolic value to express the (diachronic and synchronic) unity of the universal Church, but also because of the rich musical and artistic patrimony that these texts inspired over the centuries. This is a significant part of the world's cultural patrimony, since beauty—like truth (the faith) and goodness (morals)—is universal, or catholic, by nature. But another, almost equally serious reason for paying attention to the Latin in the Mass—apart from the fact that the Ordinary Form can be very beautiful, when celebrated in Latin, as, for example, in Pluscarden Abbey in the Diocese of Aberdeen, Scotland, where it is the norm—is the significance of the Latin language, whose literature promotes critical thinking and so is one of the bulwarks against the totalitarian tendencies of modernism.[45]

The other momentous decision Pope Benedict XVI took with implications for the reform of the reform was the setting-up of an Ordinariate for those Anglicans who

---

[45] According to Eric Voegelin, *The New Science of Politics: An Introduction* (Chicago & London: University of Chicago Press, 1952), modernity is a form of Gnosticism, which he traces back to Joachim of Fiore's speculations in the twelfth century. In its gradual undermining of Western civilization from the time of the Puritans down to our own day, the ancient classics have been instruments of critique of all forms of ideological domination disguised as progress, since they opened up the human spirit to what is not transient and so had to be eliminated if the Gnostic revolutions were to succeed (140–41). In his *Milestones: Memoirs, 1927–1977*, trans. Erasmo Leiva-Merikakis (San Francisco: Ignatius Press, 1998), 23, Ratzinger, commenting on the fact that none of his teachers of Greek and Latin had joined the Nazi Party, said: "In retrospect it seems to me that an education in Greek and Latin antiquity created a mental attitude that restricted seduction by a totalitarian ideology." Dermot Fenlon once recalls Charles Brink, the German Jewish refugee turned Anglican Professor of Latin at Cambridge, asking him in a tone of profound concern: What was the Catholic Church doing in scrapping Latin? He explained to him that the elimination of Latin was a primary objective of Hitler, as it resulted in the loss of what it means to be a free people. This was in 1968–1970, when Cambridge at the time was jettisoning both Latin and medieval history, though they seem to have reversed that trend more recently.

sought union with Rome and who were eager not to have to abandon their rich, Anglican, liturgical heritage expressed in sublime English. The resulting adaption to the Roman Missal, I am told, is very beautiful. Perhaps their new Missal can help us enrich the Ordinary Form of the Roman Rite. This might happen in a way similar to the way in which elements of the Orthodox Divine Liturgy have enriched the liturgy of the Monastic Fraternities of Jerusalem.[46]

Ours is a time of opportunity and, as ever, a time of hope. The divine liturgy is at the heart of the Church and her mission to save mankind, a mankind that is in the process of forgetting God and, so, descending into chaos and nihilism. The liturgy must be so formed and celebrated to enable contemporary man to experience God in a world that is becoming increasingly secular (and that not only in Europe or America). Since the dynamics of rituals are part of our DNA as human beings, our capacity for ritual is never entirely destroyed. That is a source of genuine hope, both for the Church and for the liturgy, once we face up to the inherent weaknesses of both the Ordinary Form and the Extraordinary Form of the Roman Rite.[47] But improving the rituals of the liturgy will take time and discernment, provided they are allowed to develop organically.[48]

---

[46] I once attended the Jerusalem Community's very beautiful Thursday Evening Liturgy in the Church of Saints Gervaise et Prothèse in Paris. It combined familiarity with deep reverence, a touch of the sublime. The same Orthodox influence is to be found in the liturgy of the contemplative Sisters of Bethlehem, on the Kinderalm in the Archdiocese of Salzburg, Austria, which convent follows the Rule of Saint Bruno.

[47] That said, the evident attraction of the Extraordinary Form today, even to the younger generation in the secular West, is a proof of the way authentic, sacred ritual resonates with our basic humanity and its fundamental need for the Transcendent.

[48] See Ratzinger's review of *The Organic Development of Liturgy: The Principles of Liturgical Reform and Their Relation to the Twentieth-Century Liturgical Movement*, by Alcuin Reid, O.S.B. (San Francisco: Ignatius Press, 2005), where he outlines his own criteria for liturgical renewal (reprinted in his *JRCW* 11:589–94).

And, of course, the real dynamics (δυναμις) of liturgy is the Holy Spirit, who continues to bring order out of the chaos caused by our often-blundering attempts to reform the liturgy ever old, ever new.

The continual reform and perfection of the liturgy is an urgent necessity in this new historical epoch in order to enable the Church, the Body of Christ, to accomplish her mission in every race and tongue and nation: to bring God's joy into our world.[49] In doing so, she is in the process of becoming more truly Catholic, which should find its highest expression in the divine liturgy that is substantially one and the same all over the world yet is expressed in diverse ritual forms, which still retain in substance the basic form of the Roman Rite. That, it seems to this writer, was the aim of the Second Vatican Council—and of Joseph Ratzinger/Pope Benedict XVI:

> When the world in all its parts has become a liturgy of God, when, in its reality, it has become adoration, then it will have reached its goal and will be safe and sound. This is the ultimate goal of St. Paul's apostolic mission as well as of our own mission. The Lord calls us to this ministry. Let us pray at this time that he may help us to carry it out properly, to become true liturgists of Jesus Christ. Amen.[50]

[49] Pope Benedict XVI, Homily at the Mass for the inauguration of his Petrine ministry, April 24, 2005.

[50] Homily on the Solemnity of Saints Peter and Paul, 2008.

APPENDIX

Sacred Chant

Fontgombault, near Poitiers, a daughter abbey of Solesmes, had surpassed its Mother Abbey in its reputation for Gregorian chant of the purest kind when I visited it in 1974. Crowds came at weekends to attend the Divine Office and High Mass. But to appreciate the chant at its most sublime, one had to attend Matins around 5:00 A.M. Alone in the ancient twelfth-century abbey church (rebuilt lovingly in the nineteenth century after falling victim to the violence of the French Revolution), one could not help noticing how one or another of the monks would suddenly, and for no apparent reason, kneel briefly and then stand up and continue his singing. This was the secret of their extraordinary sound: the kneeling was due to a mistake they made when singing, a short act of humiliation and penance. More importantly, it helped explain the superiority of the singing precisely when no outsiders were present: for them, the singing itself *is* divine worship, the work of God, the Divine Office. They sang for God, to praise Him, to worship Him. The entire life of the community revolved around the singing of the Divine Office. The

This chapter was originally a talk given to the College Choir of Saint Patrick's College, Maynooth, on January 24, 1992. I have retained the informal style of the spoken word.

asceticism of their way of life, their manual work, silence, and contemplation prepared them for, and was nurtured by, the Divine Office. Their singing, in other words, was both a product and an expression of their spirituality, their life for and in God, for His greater Glory, as Saint Ignatius of Loyola summed up his life and work.

Saint Augustine coined the phrase: he who sings well prays twice over. But he also told his congregation of sailors, merchants, and their wives to sing a new song not only with their lips but with their lives. And he put his finger on the temptation that is characteristic of the one who either performs or listens to music in all its grandeur. As he tells us in his *Confessions*, he was so moved by the beauty of the music and singing in Milan that he was afraid of being distracted from the worship of God.

I would like to comment on the three points that Saint Augustine made and apply them to the spirituality of singing in a choir whose purpose is liturgical: *laus Deo*—the overriding theme of the architecture of the Maynooth College Chapel.

I

Singing is not only prayer set to music, but is itself, or should be, a particularly intensive form of prayer. This, of course, raises the question as to what constitutes sacred music as distinct from profane music, a question that is too broad to be considered here,[1] apart from a few comments at the end. What is important to note, however, is that, as Ratzinger has pointed out, there *is* a difference, indeed, a profound one (due to its purpose, worship of God, and to the depth of the soul that it expresses), despite

---

[1] See above, chapter 4.

the multitude of different kinds of liturgical music.[2] It is very difficult to say what exactly this difference is, since, in the final analysis, it can only be sensed by someone who is sensitive not only to music but to the spiritual realities of joy, sorrow, awe, and wonder that echo in the depth of the soul when we are touched by the Transcendent. In some almost inexpressible sense, sacred music (like sacred art) is a response to the awe and mystery of God and so appeals to the deepest recesses of our being, if one may say so, beyond reason and emotion, though experienced in them. One of the main characteristics of truly sacred music, it seems to me, is a certain self-effacement; it does not draw attention to itself. Whereas this self-effacement is common to all great art and human endeavor, it has a specific meaning in liturgical music.

It is clear that there is a subtle but important difference between a public concert and liturgy, i.e., between music performed for the enjoyment of others (and in recognition of the talent of the performers) and music whose sole aim is to give praise to God and in so doing to lift up the hearts of those who are also participating in this communal act of worship. As a result, participation on the part of either singers or listeners is deepened and should end in communion with God in silence. Since sacral music, even when performed in concert, retains some echo of this character,

---

[2] Even though in the following I may seem to refer mainly to the great Church music (Gregorian chant, polyphony, or that composed by a Mozart, Schubert, Byrd, or Fauré), I do not wish to exclude popular hymns or folk-music, much of which is also truly sacred music, and often very great. One thinks, e.g., of *Silent Night* or *Lead Kindly Light*, Negro spirituals or the very beautiful Advent and Christmas hymns from Central Europe, not to mention some fine examples from the Irish and English traditions. See Anthony Esolen, "Finally, the Bishops Talk Sense about Hymns", *Crisis Magazine*, December 22, 2020, on the report by the Doctrinal Commission of the USCCB, *Catholic Hymnody at the Service of the Church*.

it is traditional in central Europe—or at least, it used to be—*not* to applaud after such a concert of sacred music, as I experienced, e.g., in the Lutheran University Church in Münster (at a performance of Handel's *Messiah*) and in the Baroque Catholic Church in Vienna, the Karlskirche (at a performance of the sacred music of Saint Hildegard of Bingen). When the concert of Church music was over, all quietly left the Church, uplifted by the singing, touched by the sacred. And, incidentally, on both occasions the singers, too, remained out of sight, up in the choir lofts.

That may seem to have been a digression, but it brings us to the heart of the matter. Singing in church is itself a form of worship. Thus, it makes little sense to feel somehow or other that by singing in choir one is being distracted from the main object of Mass, to pray, as though prayer were limited to speaking and silent contemplation. Singing is a particularly intensive form of prayer, or it should be, to the extent that it echoes that "sacred chant which is sung without ceasing before the throne of God and the Lamb" (Pope Urban VIII).

II

Why, then, is either chant or singing *not* a form of prayer for many people? There are as many reasons as there are people. Obviously, if the singing is poor, it is more a distraction than a prayer. If the music is superficial and profane rather than sacred, profound, or sublime, if, e.g., it is too theatrical or sentimental, then the result can be a loss of the sense of awe and mystery in God's presence and so a distraction from prayer. But for those who sing in choirs, the real reason may be their failure to take Augustine's second point seriously enough: sing the new song of the sons of God with your lives rather than your lips. The saints in heaven uninterruptedly sing the heavenly liturgy. Our liturgy is a faint echo of that heavenly liturgy. To be more exact, it is a participation in it, but only partial, since we are still "on the way", imperfect pilgrims struggling to be saints.

Music, like sport or serious academic research, is a fully human activity. That means that it affects our whole lives, if we permit it. Just as sport can teach us such human virtues as self-control, fairness, comradeship, etc., so too music does, or can, do likewise. Singing in a choir itself ought to engender that self-effacement I mentioned earlier, since one has to learn to sing in harmony with others, no one voice dominating, but each singer attuned to the others and yet each making his unique contribution to the harmonious whole sound. A choir is, or should be, a symbol of that harmony which is the fruit of *caritas*.[3] So, too, the hours of practice in preparation for a Mass or a liturgical celebration are part of that worship with one's life.

III

Augustine's third point I mentioned at the opening was the temptation to be distracted from worshipping God by the sheer beauty of music in church. It is the temptation to use music for one's own satisfaction if one is a hearer,

---

[3] On his way to Rome to be thrown to the lions, the aged Bishop Ignatius of Antioch in Syria wrote to the Church in Ephesus to thank them for sending a delegation to see him in Smyrna as a sign of solidarity. In it he admonishes them to live in unity and uses an image taken from the liturgy—which would have been a sung liturgy—to depict that unity and harmony: "Hence it is fitting for you to set yourselves in harmony with the mind of the bishop, as indeed you do. For your noble presbytery, worthy of God, is fitted to the bishop, as the strings to a harp. And thus *by means of your accord and harmonious love Jesus Christ is sung. Form yourselves one and all into a choir, that blending in concord, taking the key-note of God, you may sing in unison with one voice through Jesus Christ to the Father,* that He may hear you and recognize by means of your well-doing that you are members of His Son." *Ad Eph.* 4 (trans. J.H. Srawley); see also *Ad Rom.* 2, 2 and *Ad Philad.*1, 2. The image was taken up by several Fathers of the Church, such as St. Athanasius.

or, if one is a singer, perhaps even for one's own glory, instead of God's glory. This leads us to the very heart of a spirituality for those whose liturgical function is that of the *cantores*, but in particular when one sings alone as cantor. Who is the singer trying to please; who is he trying to satisfy? Is it the congregation? If it is, then the congregation has been turned into an audience at a concert; their approval, indeed, their applause, is sought, even if only subconsciously. Above all, one must give one's full attention to *what* one is singing, the words of the psalm, hymn, or antiphon. This applies to each individual member of the choir but especially to the cantor who sings alone.

IV

We have just touched on one of the distinguishing marks of Christian liturgy: it is formed, not only by rite and symbol (which are basic), but by words, the Word of God expressed in human words. The music unlocks the meaning of the words; in a certain sense, it is subservient to them. Liturgical music has humility as one of its essential characteristics. The meaning of the words is unfolded in the best Church music; its depth is plumbed. But, for the singer, the words remain the starting point: they need to be the subject of meditation. They must, first of all, echo in the heart of the singer before they find expression through his lips if they are to echo in the hearts of the rest of the congregation. (The same, of course, applies to the lector.)

In another sense, great Church music enables us to interpret the words, enables us to grasp the depth of meaning adumbrated by the words, since music transcends words.[4]

---

[4] And words themselves can be understood as a form of music, seen (or, rather, heard) especially in poetry, where meaning and sound, the very sound of the words, complement each other.

All great music is profoundly religious, metaphysical. George Steiner comments: "In ways so obvious as to make any statement a tired cliché, yet of an undefinable and tremendous nature, music puts our being as men and women in touch with that which transcends the sayable, which outstrips the analysable.... The meanings of the meaning of music transcend."[5] But sacred music as such goes farther, that is, music specifically inspired by the rites and words of the liturgy and capable of capturing the heights and depths of the soul's encounter with God in ecstasy and ashes, joy and grief. Sacred music enables the inexplicable that is partially articulated in words to *remain* inexplicable. In some of the more sublime examples of classical Gregorian chant, the words tend to dissolve into pure sound.[6] In a sense, they transcend themselves, dissolve into the ineffable. In the liturgy, we are at the threshold between this world and the next, where the beyond bends down and enters this world, and we cross over temporarily into the beyond. Sacred music is sacred when it crosses that threshold and carries us with it. "I wept at the beauty of Your hymns and canticles, and was powerfully moved at the sweet sound of Your Church's singing. Those sounds flowed into my ears, and the truth streamed into my heart: so that my feeling of devotion overflowed, and the tears ran from my eyes, and I was happy in them."[7]

[5] George Steiner, *Real Presences: Is There Any Meaning in What We Say?* (London and Boston: Faber & Faber, 1989), 218; though this is an essay on contemporary literature, Steiner has much to say of immediate relevance not only to music but to theology and politics.

[6] It is of no little significance that Gregorian chant is the most suitable of all sacred music, since its origins are to be found in the way the Hebrew psalms were chanted in the synagogue at the time of Christ and the apostles (cf. Father Joseph Fessio, S.J., "The Mass of Vatican II", *Catholic World Report*, July 23, 2021).

[7] Saint Augustine, *Confessions*, 9,6, trans. F.J. Sheed, 2nd ed. (Indianapolis and Cambridge: Hackett, 2006), 172.

It is worth remembering that, until the twelfth century, "all Masses were sung Masses, usually solemn. With the increased demand, the external ceremonial of the Mass became simplified, and the singing was reduced first to a sort of subdued chant, and then to a simple spoken rite. Solemn High Mass remained normative, but low Masses began to multiply."[8] One of the largely unused potentials of the new Roman Missal is the provision it makes for the liturgy to be chanted—indeed, musical notes are offered for all parts of the Mass, including the Eucharistic Prayers, apart from the Readings, though the Gospel can, on special solemnities, be sung to powerful effect.[9] To provide suitable music is also a challenge to composers to be creative in a way that is completely legitimate. Perhaps the time has come to give greater attention to music's potentially enriching, but largely ignored, dimension in the dynamics of the reformed liturgy.

---

[8] Donald Prudlo, "The Feast of Corpus Christi", *New Liturgical Movement*, August 11, 2020; http://www.newliturgicalmovement.org/2020/08/the-anniversary-of-feast-of-corpus.html#.XzbebuhKjIV

[9] This is the tradition in the Seminary Chapel of Saint Patrick's College, Maynooth, on Easter Sunday morning, when the Gospel is intoned using a simple but beautiful melody, which is accompanied by the organ in the distance.

POSTSCRIPT

Ite missa est

Up to the reform of the liturgy, Mass ended with the dismissal: *Ite missa est* (to which the response is: *Deo gratias*). It is one of the most ancient Roman formulas—and, it seems, one of the most difficult to translate.[1] The mass (*missa*) is over, but the mission (*missio*) now begins—namely, to allow that love of God encountered in the divine liturgy to transform one's daily life into a life of service to one's neighbor. Without that inner transformation, every attempted reform of the liturgy is simply futile. To give the last word to Pope Benedict XVI:

> Each celebration of the Eucharist makes sacramentally present the gift that the crucified Lord made of his life, for us and for the whole world. In the Eucharist Jesus also makes us witnesses of God's compassion toward all our brothers and sisters. The eucharistic mystery thus gives rise to a service of charity toward neighbor, which "consists in the very fact that, in God and with God, I love even the person whom I do not like or even know. This can only take place on the basis of an intimate encounter with God, an encounter which has become a communion of will, affecting even my feelings. Then I learn to look on this other person not simply with my eyes and my feelings,

[1] Cf. *Ite Missa Est* | Catholic Answers, from which the following is taken.

but from the perspective of Jesus Christ" [Benedict XVI, Encyclical letter *Deus Caritas Est* (25 December 2005), 18: AAS 98 (2001)]. In all those I meet, I recognize brothers or sisters for whom the Lord gave his life, loving them "to the end" (Jn 13:1).[2]

---

[2] Pope Benedict XVI, Post-Synodal Apostolic Exhortation *Sacramentum Caritatis*, February 22, 2007.

SOURCES

Introduction: Previously unpublished.

Chapter One: "Verbum Domini: Word and Rite in Ratzinger's Sacramental Theology". In Janet E. Rutherford and James O'Brien, eds., *Benedict XVI and the Roman Missal. Proceedings of the Fourth Fota Liturgical Conference, 2011*, 9–20. Dublin and New York: Four Courts Press/ Scepter Publishers, 2013.

Chapter Two: "Benedict XVI: Pope and *Leiturgos*". In Neil J. Roy and Janet E. Rutherford, eds., *Benedict XVI and the Sacred Liturgy: Proceedings of the First Fota International Liturgy Conference*, 13–16. Dublin: Four Courts Press, 2010; reprinted in *Inside the Vatican,* May 2010, 28–29.

Chapter Three: "Sacred Space". In D. Vincent Twomey S.V.D. and Janet E. Rutherford, eds., *Benedict XVI and Beauty in Sacred Art and Architecture: Proceedings of the Second Fota International Liturgy Conference*, 15–23. Dublin: Four Courts Press, 2011.

Chapter Four: "On the Theological Basis for Church Music according to Joseph Ratzinger". In Janet Elaine Rutherford, ed., *Benedict XVI and Beauty in Sacred Music.* Dublin and New York: Four Courts Press/Scepter Publishers, 2012.

Chapter Five: "Rubrics and the Sacrificial Nature of the Eucharist". In Gerard Deighan, ed., *Celebrating the Eucharist: Sacrifice and Communion. Proceedings of the Fifth Fota International Liturgy Conference,* 249–62. Wells, Somerset: Smenos Publications, 2014.

Excursus: "What's Wrong with an Amazonian Rite?", *Catholic World Report,* May 20, 2020.

Chapter Six: Previously unpublished.

Appendix: Previously unpublished.

INDEX

Aaron, 124n13
Abel, 104
aboriginal rituals, 44–45
Abraham, 33, 104
absolution, 45–46
abstraction, 110–11
acclamation, 51
acheiropoiētos, 134
actio, 51
action, liturgical, 54, 76
action of God, 9, 47n
actions, symbolic. *See under*
  symbols/symbolism:
  symbolic actions
active participation in the
  liturgy. *See participatio actuosa*
  (active participation)
activity, overemphasis on, 99
Ad Gentes: Decree on
  Missionary Activity, 127–28
Addai, St., 121–22
adoration, 57, 98, 112, 114–15,
  154
aesthetics/aestheticism, 30n29,
  35, 65, 76, 79, 149–50. *See
  also* beauty
Africa, 22, 27, 45, 109–10, 124,
  128, 141–42; *Chihamba*
  ritual of the Ndembu tribe,
  105n21, 116n45; Zaire
  (Congo) and the Zairean
  Rite, 120–21
aggiornamento, 16–17, 132

Agnus Dei (hymn), 112, 151
Alexandria, 121, 159n
alienation, 19, 71, 89, 148n40,
  150
allegory, 41n8, 84
altar, 39, 44n16, 63, 70–72,
  75n25, 114n41, 127, 143,
  146; in Papua New Guinea,
  144n33; position of, 95n8,
  113–15
Amazonian Rite, 12, 36,
  119–28
Ambrose, St., 87
America, 18, 153. *See also* Latin
  America/Latin American
  Church
Amoris Laetitia (Francis), 119–20
angels, 62–63
Anglican Christianity, 28,
  52n35, 131n4, 152–53
anthropology of ritual. *See
  under* ritual: anthropology of
Antioch, 121, 159n
antiphons, 160
antiquity, 152n
Apocalypse (book of
  Revelation), 72–73
apostles, 57n1, 82, 161n6
applause, 88, 96, 158, 160
apse (architecture), 44n16, 142
Aquinas, St. Thomas. *See*
  Thomas Aquinas, St.
archaism, 54, 114n41

Mozarabic Rite, 122
Mozart, W.A., 88, 157n
multipurpose churches, 67
music/sacred music, 79–91,
    155–62; and architecture,
    76; instrumental, 83, 88–89;
    polyphonic, 142, 157n. *See
    also* chant, sacred; hymns;
    singing
mysterion, 43
mysterium of God, 102n16
mystery, 52; of Christ, 26, 49,
    86; of a church, 75n26;
    of the Eucharist, 48, 137,
    163; of God, 25, 157–58;
    of the liturgy, 37, 39n5,
    52, 61, 111, 121; of man's
    existence, 100; of Mass, 144,
    150; the Paschal Mystery,
    47–48. *See also* silence
mysticism, 60, 72–73, 84, 141;
    Eucharist as mystical heart
    of Christianity, 137
myth, 44, 47, 101, 103, 124

nations, 22
nature religions, 47n, 102–4
Nazism, 96n8, 152n
Ndembu tribe, *Chihamba* ritual
    of, 105n21, 116n45
neo-clericalism. *See
    under* clericalism: and
    neo-clericalism
neoliberalism, 21
Neoscholasticism, 39, 70, 140
"The New Pagans and the
    Church" (Ratzinger), 16–17
New Testament. *See under*
    Scripture: New Testament
new world, 132

Nicaea II, Council of (787),
    69, 74
Nietzsche, Friedrich, 100
nihilism, 153
noble simplicity. *See* simplicity
nomads, 114
non-Christian philosophy and
    religion, 18, 23, 27, 32, 116
Nostra Aetate: Declaration
    on the Relation of the
    Church to Non-Christian
    Religions, 23

obedience, 55, 71, 94, 96, 112;
    inner attitude of, 145–47
O'Brien, James, Monsignor,
    11–12
O'Callaghan, Michael, 79
Offertory, 97, 115, 142
Office, Divine, 10–11, 155–56
Old Testament. *See under*
    Scripture: Old Testament
Order of Mass, 112
Ordinary Form of the Roman
    Rite, 53, 62–63, 97,
    111–15, 130, 138, 141–45,
    148–53
Ordinary of the Mass, 151
ordination, 79, 124n13, 126–27,
    140n27, 143
Oriental Catholic Churches,
    120–23
Oriental Rites, 121–22
orientation, 43, 72, 102, 150
Origen, 49
Orthodox Christianity, 28,
    34n34, 69, 84–85, 131,
    140n27, 153
orthodoxia (a life of "right
    worship"), 117